Jesus in Isolation

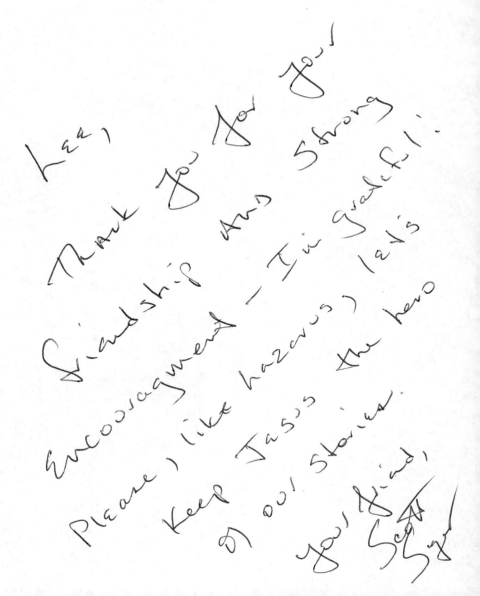

Lea,

Thank you for your friendship and strong encouragement — I'm grateful. Please, like hazardous lab's Keep Jesus the hero of our stories.

Your friend,
Scott

Jesus in Isolation

Lazarus, Viruses, and Us

by W. SCOTT SAGER

WIPF & STOCK · Eugene, Oregon

JESUS IN ISOLATION
Lazarus, Viruses, and Us

Wipf & Stock
An Imprint of Wipf and Stock Publishers
199 W. 8th Ave., Suite 3
Eugene, OR 97401

www.wipfandstock.com

PAPERBACK ISBN: 978-1-7252-9511-7
HARDCOVER ISBN: 978-1-7252-9512-4
EBOOK ISBN: 978-1-7252-9513-1

03/03/21

To Mom, Dad, and Suzanne

Jesus had, as his nearest and dearest family,
Mary, Martha, and Lazarus.
Gratefully, I have the three of you,
with Suzanne as my best and closest friend.

Contents

PART TWO

Introduction

A Microscopic Killer Gone Viral

[Jesus] came to this world and became a man in order to spread to other men the kind of life He has—by what I call "good infection." Every Christian is to become a little Christ. The whole purpose of becoming a Christian is simply nothing else.

—C. S. Lewis

Isolation. It's God's gift most of us never wanted. And quite frankly, we're tired of it now.

During the 2020 COVID-19 global pandemic our entire civilization has been in isolation; we see its effects daily in nursing homes, in ER wards, in the unemployment lines, on bank statements, and, most sadly, in newspaper obituaries. Ours is what C. S. Lewis called a "grief observed"—but uniquely this grief is being experienced in isolation, all alone. The social distancing, self-isolation, quarantine, and hygiene protocols have not stopped the decimation brought upon communities, churches, small businesses, and major metropolitan areas. People are getting infected by the virus, and while some show no symptoms at all, others soon find themselves in a hospital ER on oxygen and a ventilator. Many never come off. The world watches on in a collective grief—but watches suspended in personal isolation.

Coronavirus disease 2019 (COVID-19) is an infectious disease first identified in December 2019 in Wuhan, the capital of China's Hubei province—a city of over twelve million people. The virus is primarily spread between people during close contact, often via small droplets produced

1

by coughing, sneezing, and talking. From Wuhan, the virus mutated into at least five strains and as a viral contagion has spread globally, resulting in an ongoing pandemic the world has not seen since the Spanish Flu of 1918. The viral pandemic is accountable for more deaths than will ever be known, as well as the cratering of economies around the world, resulting in lay-offs, financial ruin, and the economic collapse of nations, states, and civil governments. As the entire world deals with "loss" of every kind, a universal and collective grief is observed. COVID-19 has left no one un-touched—and has left no one *not* feeling alone.

Attempts are now underway to ascertain the exact cause and origina-tion of this viral contagion that has decimated the planet from Afghanistan to Zimbabwe and all points in between. Most theories involve a wild horse-shoe bat as the unaffected carrier of the virus; the dreaded evil contagion lived inside the bat without affect. But the virus somehow spread from the bat to "patient zero," who originated the spread among humans. The trans-mission could have occurred in the wild, or through a failure to observe biosafety protocols during research of the virus in one of two infectious disease labs in Wuhan. Many think the spread began to multiply through contact at a wet market in Wuhan.

Although we may never know the origin of the viral contagion CO-VID-19, we do know from whence it originated. The first violation of safety standards occurred not in a lab in Wuhan, but in a garden somewhere in modern Iraq, between the rivers Tigris and Euphrates. From there a ser-pent, later called Satan, infected Adam as "patient zero" with the deadly disease called "sin." The consequences of that act brought forth a viral set of contagions of various strains that infected the entire human race with a spiritual virus filled with physical, emotional, social, and spiritual con-sequences, resulting in sure and certain death for all mankind. No one could stand up to the disease, and there was no known cure. It all started there with Adam as "patient zero" and Eve as the first to receive the spread. Through them we have all received sin's viral contagion, and death is the grim result apart from a vaccine.

Nothing mankind could do served as a vaccine to stem the continued spread of the virus. The curve continued to spike and the global infection rate neared 100 percent. Jesus entered the world as the God-man and as God the Father's response to the human condition. He did not come dressed in a hazmat suit with an n-95 mask and protective shield, but wrapped in rags and lying in a manger. C.S. Lewis explains it best in saying that Jesus "came to this world and became a man in order to spread to other men the kind of life He has—by what I call '*good infection*.' Every Christian is to become a little Christ. The whole purpose of becoming a Christian is simply nothing else."[1]

Jesus came that an antidote stronger than the virus could be ours through the vaccine of becoming one with Christ—a little Christ. The apostle Paul explains it this way, "We always carry around in our body the death of Jesus, so that the life of Jesus may also be revealed in our body. For we who are alive are always being given over to death for Jesus' sake, so that his life may be revealed in our mortal body" (2 Cor 4:10–11).

This is the story of how Jesus takes away the bad infection and replaces it with himself as the good infection. It happens in isolation, but to bring the good infection to the entire human race. Through the story of Jesus and Lazarus we find our own isolation is far more than merely a nuisance; we find through Jesus' own isolation that it is part of the cure. Through his own isolation, Jesus takes upon himself the sickness of us all; he absorbs it as his own.

The story of the death of Lazarus is a monumental moment in the ministry of Jesus. Jesus is the primary actor. He, not Lazarus, is the focal point of the story, for only he can absorb the incredible grief of this broken world—and heal the virus infecting us all. This story is the weightiest of all Jesus' biblical encounters with people—and is monumental in John's Gospel. It serves as a signpost pointing to Jesus' cross, an exit ramp concluding his three-year ministry and also a window into the ways of God in the midst of our suffering.

This is your invitation to join Jesus where *sickness*, *death*, *grief*, and *isolation* take center stage. Perhaps no other story in the life of Jesus speaks to our COVID-19 world like this one does. *Jesus in Isolation* is thirteen chapters to give you time to ponder the movements made in the biblical account. The church fathers have been consulted wherever possible, bringing to bear nearly two thousand years of church history. The thirteen chapters also help to serve churches and small groups interested in important conversations geared to foster greater discipleship. At the end of each chapter a poem has been selected as a significant glimpse into the deep drama within every chapter. Most churches have preachers, priests, and parishioners but often lack poets. In the world of Twitter, Instagram, and email, God's people long for the perspective of the poet—without even realizing it.

Throughout this book I have worked diligently to remain faithful to the biblical text. At the same time, I have attempted to fill in the gaps in the narrative through "sanctified imagination."[2] My goal has been to crawl inside the text and describe the sights, sounds, and smells I find inside after thousands of hours spent walking the streets of Jerusalem and Bethany. The hope is that the biblical witness will come alive for you as well. This method of reading Scripture was common among the earliest Christians living with an oral tradition. It was later described as a way of meditation by Teresa of Avila in *The Interior Castle* and made popular by the preaching of my hero, Peter Marshall, and my friend Max Lucado.

Unimaginable moments of grief lie ahead for every believer—it is an unavoidable part of Christian living. That said, we need to live in that space well, as the world observes our isolation and our grief. But we live in that space also knowing that in Jesus, our grief has been more than observed—it has been absorbed into himself. Jesus "has borne our sorrows and carried our grief" and only through him do we discover a sense of healing and hope. May this book help you make sense of COVID, and to spread the "good infection" as well.

—W. Scott Sager (Easter, 2020)

MEDITATION I

> Variable, and therefore miserable condition of man!
> this minute I was well, and am ill, this minute.
> I am surprised with a sudden change,
> and alteration to worse, and can impute it to no cause,
> nor call it by any name.
> We study health, and we deliberate upon our meats,
> and drink, and air, and exercises,
> and we hew and we polish every stone
> that goes to that building; and so
> our health is a long and a regular work:
> but in a minute a cannon batters all,
> overthrows all, demolishes all;
> a sickness unprevented for all our diligence,
> unsuspected for all our curiosity;
> nay, undeserved, if we consider only disorder,
> summons us, seizes us,
> possesses us, destroys us in an instant.
> O miserable condition of man!

—John Donne (1572–1631)[3]

CHAPTER ONE

David's Cry Heard 'Round the World[4]

The central idea of the great part of the Old Testament may be called the idea of the loneliness of God.

—G. K. CHESTERTON

They took Absalom's body, threw it into a big pit in the forest and piled up a heap of rocks over him.

—2 SAM 18:17

RAPE, INCEST, AND A palace coup all came crashing down on David— the king "after God's own heart." How did things get so dysfunctional so quickly?

The vanquished king, chased from his palace, gathered a few of his belongings and flung them into an animal skin. He then rushed out the palace doors and into self-isolation, leaving ten wives behind to care for the place. The once regal king hardly paused to think of all the marvelous moments he had there over the last quarter of a century. His children were born and raised there; his kingdom had grown in fame and recognition so that the entire world came to visit and gain an audience with him. "If not for that day on the roof," he muttered, "surely none of this would be happening right now . . ."

He tossed the bag upon the steed and fled the city as a bloodless coup became his undoing. The soldiers still faithful to him escorted him from the city and through the Kidron Valley. As his white stallion made its way up the Mount of Olives, the king popped the reigns lightly and his horse began the steep climb to the top. The rebellion gave the king more pain than an enemy could ever inflict. It was his son leading the revolt—he had won the hearts and minds of the people right out from under his father's nose. "How could this be?" he wondered aloud, really not addressing his thoughts to anyone in particular. How far the king had fallen in just a few short years.

This rebellion traced its roots back to his own ill-fated decision to skip the spring battles and stay back in his own self-induced isolation in Jerusalem with the women, children and older men. *If only I had stayed in the battle I could have avoided the temptation that ensnared me,* he thought. But he didn't. He didn't, because he didn't want to at the time. He was tired, bored, and a bit weary and looking for something new, young, and exciting. He found it in Bathsheba, the gorgeous woman with the alluring figure bathing unaware on the rooftop. He leaned in to look. He lusted and longed for an encounter.

He called. She came. He slept with her. She went home. That was supposed to be "the end of the story." But it was a note a month later that messed up everything: "Pregnant. Baby is yours. What do we do now? — Bathsheba." The king called the woman's husband home from the battle-front to sleep with his wife and cover it all up. But he declined a night with his wife in order to honor his comrades still fighting at the front. Even when the king got him drunk, his moral fiber surpassed the king's when sober. So the king sent the distinguished soldier back to the front line with a secret message for the general in charge: "Make sure Uriah is a casualty of war today."

The king made sure everyone observed his grief. He even came out smelling like a rose when he did the "honorable thing" and married the fallen soldier's bride. To everyone outside the palace walls the king's actions in taking a pregnant wife of a fallen warrior as his own was the ultimate "I support the troops" moment. The cover-up worked to perfection. . . . Until the day Nathan the prophet showed his face. After a story about herds of sheep and a precious ewe lamb, Nathan pointed his finger directly in the king's face and said the words the king could not shake and had never, ever forgotten: "David, you are the man!"

His sin had found him out—and the consequences of his actions would haunt him as long as he lived. What Nathan had spoken then was now being fulfilled as the king fled the palace after the rebellion began:

> Out of your own household I am going to bring calamity upon you. Before your very eyes I will take your wives and give them to one who is close to you, and he will lie with your wives in broad daylight. You did it in secret, but I will do the thing in broad daylight before all Israel. (2 Sam 12:11–12)

First, Amnon had raped his sister Tamar. Then Absalom had killed his brother Amnon in revenge. Absalom then lived as a fugitive for three years. Returning to Jerusalem, Absalom worked behind the scenes to steal the kingdom from his father. Absalom now held the palace, and David was forced into a type of quarantine. It seemed grief upon grief had been piled on his head.

Arriving at the top of the Mount of Olives, David paused to look down and survey his royal city one last time before going into hiding. From high above on the hill, Jerusalem looked beautiful and majestic. There were the tabernacle and the ark. There were the walls and the garrisons. There was his palace—the one he had built for himself. And there was his son Absalom up on the roof. What was the son who had stolen the kingdom now doing on the roof, he wondered? He asked one of the soldiers for his field glasses—he wanted to take a closer look. When he put the glasses up to his eye, he was unprepared for the flood of emotions that surged within him. It was Absalom all right, and he was on the roof systematically raping the ten wives David had left behind—in broad daylight!

In that moment, David's grief for a wayward son magnified exponentially until he could stand it no longer. Mustering all his strength, he let out a bloodcurdling cry that could be heard across the mountain tops: *"Eloi, Eloi, lama sabachthani?"*

Everyone observed his grief. And he kept repeating those words over and over again as they led him into hiding—"My God, my God, why have you forsaken me?" Perhaps it was later that night while sitting in his tent not far from a crackling fire that he penned the opening verses now known as Psalm 22. It was David's manifesto on grief, suffering, and the feelings of utter abandonment and isolation that so often accompany real pain. Only one living in the darkest valley of grief could pen a psalm as deep and despairing as the one he began to compose that night.

He wrote as one whose close-by God was now far, far away. He wrote as a man whose prayers that once reached heaven's throne now weren't making it to the roof of the tent. He wrote as one crying for answers only to receive nothing but silence in return. He wrote as one who had seen God come to the aid of others, but felt stood up and kicked to the curb himself. He wrote as one whose strength was zapped, whose hope was gone, and who despaired of life. He wrote as one in isolation, completely alone no matter how many soldiers swirled in and out of camp around him. He was depressed; he was beaten down; he was empty. He was in a self-preserving exile of aloneness. His grief had no place to go.

In that emptiness he formulated his thoughts: "My God, my God, why have you forsaken me?" God was "far away" from saving him, even far from hearing "the words of his groaning." The God enthroned in heaven, who delivered his fathers when they trusted, was not coming to his aid. Instead, he was being taunted and ridiculed. Enemies surrounded him on every side; his strength was dried up and he was a shell of himself, unwilling to eat or drink. As he languished in dark despair and grief, others were arguing over his clothes and casting lots for his finest jackets. Yet there was something still there, a glimmer of hope that God would still rescue him. One day he hoped God would do something to relieve the grief.

But before things would ever get better, they were going to get far worse. Because nothing brings a grief that stings like the death of a child . . .

Absalom, his son with the beautiful hair and the Herculean physique, wasn't satisfied to rule the kingdom, possess the palace and pillage the poor wives David had left behind. His father, King David, had to be destroyed and disposed of once and for all. So the battle cry soon went out, and the rebel king mustered a massive army to fight against their former commander. The men of Israel were siding against David, and with his son Absalom, and this was only adding to David's grief.

Battle lines were drawn and all Israel was soon divided between King David the old man and King Absalom his handsome and beloved son. As soldiers began marching out into battle, Absalom was there to rally his troops with a call to show no mercy and crush the infidels.

King David on the other hand, called in his generals. He gave them the oddest of battle instructions: "Be gentle with the young man Absalom for my sake." All the troops heard the king giving the generals these orders concerning Absalom. The battle took place in the forests of Ephraim that day. Brother fought against brother, and father against son. The battle spread out over the whole countryside. The forest itself killed as many as were slain by the sword. David's men defeated the army of Israel under Absalom with casualties far beyond twenty thousand men.

Soldiers are trained in the art of war—military precision, hand-to-hand combat, and killing the enemy. Going easy on opposing forces trying to kill you, and treating their leader with kid gloves, is not what soldiers or generals are trained to do. It's not what they signed on for either. As Absalom saw the battle tide turning away from him, he fled on a mule through the thick brush of the forest. As the beast went under the thick branches of a large oak, Absalom's hair was caught in the tree. The mule kept running, leaving his master dangling from the tree by his hair. And thus the words of Moses were fulfilled, "Cursed is any man who is left hanging on a tree" (Deut 21:23).

Soon a soldier of David's happened upon the piñata king dangling by his hair and reported the situation to his commander Joab. When the soldier explained what he saw, the commander was enraged: "What! You saw him? Why didn't you strike him to the ground right there? If you had I would have given you money and a warrior's belt on the spot!" But the soldier explained, "We all heard what the king asked of you regarding his son. If word got back that I had done this deed the king's displeasure would have followed me all my life."

So Joab left to finish the job himself. Taking three javelins in his hand he plunged them into the heart of Absalom while he was still alive in the tree. Then ten of Joab's most loyal soldiers surrounded Absalom and struck him down with swords. Immediately Joab then sounded the trumpet of victory and called the troops to return to camp. They took Absalom's body and hurled it into a deep pit in the forest and piled large rocks upon it. There would be no funeral for the dead king, and no last viewing for a father who loved him so much. King David wasn't there when Absalom died, and he wasn't there for the burial. War affords no time or place for proper burials. When Absalom died, no one grieved for the dead king—at least not yet.[5]

A herald was then sent from Joab back to camp with a one-word message for the king—"Victory!" When the king received it, he followed up with a single question: "What of Absalom?" A second herald arrived with the chilling words, "May all your enemies be to you as that young man is this day." Upon hearing the news, the king was shaken to his core with grief greater than he imagined possible. He went to his room over the gateway and began to weep and wail.

As he went, he cried out: "O my son Absalom! My son, my son
Absalom! If only I had died instead of you—O Absalom, my son,
my son!" (2 Sam 18:33)

Turning towards the mountain of the Lord this father who had lost
a beloved son in the cruelest of fashions bellowed the echoing words of
inconsolable grief, *"Eloi, Eloi, lama sabachthani?"* They were still echoing
through the canyons over a thousand years later. . . . Nothing could absorb
them.

PSALM 22:1–2

My God, my God, why have you forsaken me?
  Why are you so far from saving me,
  so far from my cries of anguish?
My God, I cry out by day, but you do not answer,
  by night, but I find no rest . . .

—King David (c. 1035–970 BC)

PART ONE

Now a man named Lazarus was sick. He was from Bethany, the village of Mary and her sister Martha. ² (This Mary, whose brother Lazarus now lay sick, was the same one who poured perfume on the Lord and wiped his feet with her hair.) ³ So the sisters sent word to Jesus, "Lord, the one you love is sick."

—JOHN 11:1–3

CHAPTER TWO

Isolation and Sacred Distancing

A friend loves at all times, and adversity is made for a brother. . . .
As iron sharpens iron, so one man sharpens another. . . . There is
a friend who will stick closer to you than a brother. (Prov 17:17;
27:17)

To influence, you must love. To love, you must pray.
—Forbes Robinson

WHO WAS JESUS' "BEST Friend Forever"—his BFF? Did Jesus even have
someone to call a "best friend"?

Many never stop to consider Solomon's wise words about friends and
friendship. How might they apply to Jesus? Who was Jesus' friend that
loved at all times? Who was Jesus' brother born for adversity? Where could
Jesus turn to be sharpened as iron sharpens iron? Who was Jesus' sound-
ing board? Who was it that Jesus could go to about the troubles of a very
complicated life? Who was closer to him than any of his brothers?

One thing was for certain: Jesus couldn't really go home. If there was
a quarantine and Jesus was asked to "stay in place," home was not the place
for him to stay. He couldn't go back to Nazareth and kick up his feet, pull
out the family games, finish a puzzle, and get some rest and relaxation. His
mother didn't know what to do with him—even though she loved him.
Jesus' brothers, on the other hand, were antagonistic and adversarial. Jesus'
family dynamics during his ministry called not for a legion of angels but a
legion of counselors. His brothers were out to get him during most of his
ministry years.

13

So where did Jesus go to find a friend that sticks closer than a brother? Who could be the iron that would sharpen his, or the one made for adversity that would always be there? Where could Jesus go when he couldn't ever really go "home"?

Most readers of Scripture cede the honored place as Jesus' best friend to John the apostle. John was the one always there for Jesus. He went places with Jesus no one else went. He was closer to the heart and mind of Jesus than anyone else. John was with Jesus in the garden, John was with Jesus at his trial, John was there at the cross, and John was there at the empty tomb. John is the only one of the apostles church tradition tells us didn't die a martyr's death. John was asked by Jesus from the cross to care for his mother Mary—and we assume he did right up to her dying day. So you might be ready to say John was that best of friends for the earthly Jesus. That would be right, but not totally.

It's actually John the apostle, who wrote a Gospel,⁶ who introduces us to someone else. As close as John was to his Lord and friend Jesus, it is still John who points to another and says, "That man was Jesus' friend." And that friend was part of a family Jesus loved very much. They were his second family. The family lived in Bethany⁷ on the outskirts of Jerusalem. It was a two-mile walk from Bethany over the Mount of Olives down to the temple. And thus Jesus probably showed up at their house at least three times a year for Passover, Pentecost, and the Feast of Booths. He would spend quality time, family time, with them. There in Bethany, Jesus could "stay in place," kick up his heels, and begin to talk, share, laugh, and tease. This was the loving family Jesus' own four brothers and several sisters had never really been for him.

You may recall the two sisters in Jesus' adopted family, Mary and Martha, and the great care they took of Jesus. You might remember how one day Martha was complaining because she took immense pride in a meal for Jesus, while Mary weaseled out. Martha wanted relief from her lazy sister. That day Jesus was at their house, and he and Mary thought they all were just relaxing and enjoying time together. But Martha, the hospitable one, was trying to make sure that everything was just right for Jesus. She was going to meticulous detail to see that Jesus was honored by the food they would eat, and the decorations on the table. All the while Martha labored, Mary was sitting in the living room chatting it up with Jesus, not involved at all in any of the preparations (those younger sisters!). In Mary's mind there was no need to put on airs. Jesus was "one of us"; he could make himself at home. Martha wanted things to be beautiful and memorable—fabulous if possible. Mary just wanted to sit and chat.[8] And Jesus agreed with Mary, basically saying, "I'd much rather sit and chat, Martha, than have you be hospitable but distant."

But there was a third somebody in that home Jesus was closer to than his two adopted sisters. The propriety of Jesus, and the culture of the day, demanded Jesus have a better relationship with the man of the house than with the sisters residing there. This friend of Jesus was named Lazarus. The name "Lazarus" means "God helps," and perhaps no person in all of Scripture lived into his name quite as well. Lazarus and Jesus bonded—they were like brothers. Maybe it was the fact that they were each presumably older. Or perhaps it was the apparent fact they both were left responsible for taking care of siblings when their fathers died early.[9] We don't know exactly what it was that drew them together, but everyone could tell Jesus and Lazarus had a deep bond. Lazarus was Jesus' own "brother from another mother."

Permit yourself to imagine Jesus and Lazarus sitting late at night, sipping some of Martha's warm tea. They talked about life. In the protection and seclusion of this safe house Jesus could discuss items with Lazarus he couldn't even mention around the apostle John. He could share some challenging, and often amusing, situations with the disciples. Peter's latest foot-in-mouth episode could be laughed off here. There were the Zebedee boys asking to call down fire from heaven. Then emerged the tug-of-war going on over who among the apostles deserved to be greatest. There were frustrations that he was having with his brothers—even his mother. There was the growing disdain and apparent danger arising at the hands of the religious leaders. With Lazarus at Bethany, Jesus could talk about God's word and his own family dynamics. And Lazarus was Jesus' lookout for Jerusalem. Lazarus could tell him the news about the Holy City and what was happening at the temple. And so Lazarus and Jesus became fast friends. One is left to wonder if they wrote each other letters, or how often they kept in touch. But there was clearly something about their relationship that was so tender and meaningful that the sisters noticed it, and recognized these two had a deep bond.

Nobody knows how it happened, but something serious occurred and Lazarus became extremely sick. Maybe it was around February, during the rainy season, and Lazarus was out in the cold and wet and caught a chill. Perhaps he was in the market and there picked up a virus. As the sole provider for his family, he had nowhere else to turn and could not slow down to be ill. He tried to push through it like he did as a younger man—surely he was stronger than a virus. The sisters heard him say, "I won't let this illness get me down; I'll be okay." But the more he labored and toiled, the sicker he became. There was a persistent cough, fever, and chills—and shortness of breath like he had never encountered before. One moment he had chills, the next a high fever. His breathing was becoming erratic. They became worried and sent for a doctor, and the doctor soon announced, "Lazarus is a very sick man." But there was no such things as an ER in Bethany, no plasma therapy, and no such thing as a ventilator.

This physician's diagnosis, "Lazarus is sick," was a more in-depth prognosis than might first be realized. The doctor was noting Lazarus was not the way he was supposed to be—not the way God designed him to be. Something was wrong, and a contaminant had injected illness into the place where God had breathed life. Lazarus was not the way he was designed to be. He had been infected *with* something. He had been infected *by* someone. There was a cause and effect for what happened to Lazarus.

Months earlier, Jesus was teaching in a Capernaum home, packed to overflowing with interested listeners of this amazing rabbi. People were crammed into the doorways and jammed into the window sills, all just wanting to be within earshot of Jesus' message. That day four buddies arrived a bit late for the meeting, but with a good excuse. They had gone to fetch a dear friend who was paralyzed, placed him on a makeshift gurney, and carried him to the gospel meeting. Yet once they arrived, they were soon in despair. There was no way to get their friend close enough to Jesus for healing to occur. They were about to give up and go home, but one of the friends had a righteous/rebellious streak. He suggested they go up on the roof, tear a hole in the thatch, and drop the paralyzed guy down through the hole to meet Jesus. The friends probably replied as sane people would: "That's crazy and destroys property—we'll get in trouble." But the righteous rebel looked at his paralyzed friend and said, "It's crazy enough to work—and imagine the laughs we'll get over it in years to come!"

So the four friends took their paralyzed buddy up on the roof, tore through the straw and stubble, dug through the tar and pitch, peeled back the lower layer of sticks, and made a vast opening in a rich neighbor's ceiling. Then they lowered their friend by ropes down into the presence of Jesus. Imagine all they were willing to do to get their friend into the presence of Jesus—this boldness Jesus soon would call "faith." Once the man was lowered down just in front of Jesus, the rabbi, who was also nicknamed "the Great Physician," gave his prognosis of the paralyzed man who dropped in on them. Looking him over from head to toe, Jesus uttered his prescription, "Young man, your sins are forgiven."

Imagine what the four young men on the roof must have yelled when they heard those words. "No, Jesus!" they could have shouted in unison; "We want you to heal him." And heal him Jesus soon would, but healing would be for the minor diagnosis. The major diagnosis, from Jesus' point of view, was that this man had been injected with sin. And sin was now the virus that was killing him.[10]

The Bible, and Jesus for that matter, take it for granted that people are sin-filled. Starting with Adam, all become infected with the stain and soil of sin. It's not the human genome that tells what will eventually kill a person, but sin. Sin has ruined every thing, and keeps every human from living the good life. Every human, not just Lazarus, is no longer the way they were designed to be. Many may want to blame nature, blame disease, or blame genetics—but Jesus encouraged his disciples to place the ultimate blame on the shoulders where it belongs. It is Satan's doing.[11]

Lazarus was sick, in more ways than one. So the sisters forced Lazarus to self-quarantine in his room; he went into isolation. Meanwhile, Mary and Martha began to do their thing. Martha went to boil water and Mary went to get some blankets. They were scurrying around the house doing whatever they could to help, when they bumped into each other in the hall-way. At the exact same moment they turned to each other and said, "I wish Jesus were here. If Jesus were here, everything would be okay!"

The sisters brought their basin, towels, hot water, and warm tea in to the doctor, and then they sat. Sat still. They were in the waiting room of life—forced to sit in isolation as life and death matters swirled all around them. Nothing was left for them to do but wait. Soon they looked up to see Lazarus, so weak he could barely motion. Yet he was giving them the "come here" signal with his finger. The sisters cozied up to Lazarus and put their ears close to his mouth. There they heard him audibly whisper, "Where is Jesus?" Hearing their brother's desperate cry, the sisters knew for certain Lazarus was at death's door. Lazarus's life was at that boundary between life and death—and wisely, he wanted Jesus to be there self-quarantined with him.

Lazarus knew any moment, any deep breath, might be his last. And it is here, at this point, that our Bibles pick up in John 11. Mary and Martha decided they had to get word to Jesus. Wherever he was at the moment, Jesus needed to know about his closest friend. It was a matter of life and death. Asking around, the sisters discovered Jesus was a day away near the Jordan River. The sisterly duo then sat down and reasoned, "Okay, let's send for a messenger and let's get a word to Jesus, because this message has to absolutely, positively get there overnight."

What did the message say? Mary wanted to write: "Jesus, help—Stop—Lazarus is dying—Stop." But Martha counseled, "Are you sure we can write that? I mean, is that really fair? You know in Jerusalem there are people plotting to kill Jesus. And if we ask him to come back here, aren't we asking him to sign his own death certificate? Aren't we asking him to put himself back in harm's way? Is there any way we can say, 'Come quickly' to Jesus knowing that he will probably get killed for coming?"

But the more they thought about it, the more they realized they had to tell Jesus something. Lazarus wanted him to know. Jesus had the right to know—and he would want to know about this matter of life and death. The sisters reasoned Jesus would be very disappointed if they did not tell him everything. They began to talk it through and realized, "You know what? We don't have to beg Jesus to come. Let's just lay the facts out and trust Jesus to do what is right and best."

Martha looked at the situation and marveled, "Why should we beg Jesus to do what love will compel him to do anyway?" And so this is the message they sent:

> Jesus, the one you love is sick.
> Signed, Mary and Martha.

And after they sent the messenger off, something amazing happened. The very moment the messenger left the house, there was a peace about their situation that hadn't been there before. This indescribable peace was guarding their hearts and minds; something had changed in them. Simply inviting Jesus into their situation had stirred their hearts and calmed their spirits. They began to realize how all their efforts to help and to heal had only placed Lazarus in their little hands. Finally, they had decided to put Lazarus in the far-larger hands of Jesus, who kept his own hands in the hands of God. And through that effort there was now a peace that surpassed all understanding that hadn't been there before. The women slept well for the first time in weeks, and they awoke the next day to take even better care of Lazarus at the most challenging hour of his life.

Pain and isolation would bring Lazarus, Mary, and Martha closer to Jesus and his Father than anything else ever could. In that regard, the virus had done them a favor. Jesus had whispered and laughed with the three in their pleasures and had spoken with them in daily cares. But pain was the megaphone God would use to rouse a deaf world and bring the two sisters to their knees. Lazarus's pain and suffering would usher them into a new desperation, a new reality of the human condition, and a new resiliency to depend upon God because nothing else would do. A later follower of Jesus who lost his wife to a cruel cancer, C. S. Lewis, once explained, "Pain insists on being attended to. God whispers in our pleasures, speaks in our conscience, but shouts in our pain; it is his megaphone to rouse a deaf world."[12] And the sisters' way of attending to God's rousing megaphone was to send a petitionary telegram (of prayer) to Jesus.

The sisters had no need to send a telegram to Jesus unless they honestly wanted their situation to change, and believed Jesus could do something about it. When Jesus gave his followers the "Lord's Prayer" his phrase "thy Kingdom come, thy will be done" was never meant to be an excuse for impotent prayers. Using "thy will be done" as an excuse to never tell God what is really wanted is not the way of Jesus. If all the sisters had truly wanted to say to Jesus was that they hoped God's will would occur, they never would have sent the telegram. Yet many followers of Jesus in later days have ceased to pray for exactly the same reason. "Thy will be done" is what is said *after* one tells God, through Jesus, what is deeply felt and urgently wanted. Even in the garden of Gethsemane, Jesus first pleaded with God for what he deeply and urgently wanted to be God's will—only afterwards adding, "But not my will but yours be done." Those who pray best, pray first for what they earnestly, deeply, ardently want to be God's will. They know there is no shame in begging that the longings of their hearts can be effective in shaping the will of Almighty God.

The sisters' telegram to Jesus was a statement of faith. It was sent believing that Jesus had a capacity to do more for Lazarus than what family or friends, physicians or prescriptions could ever do. Somehow, Jesus could absorb the anxiety and worry of the sisters and give them a peace. Without realizing it, the sisters were embracing Jesus as the Suffering Servant of Isaiah 53 who would, in the end, "bear the sins of many and make intercessions for those in need." Through their telegram, Jesus had become their advocate and intercessor—the one who would hear their deepest concerns and pass them along as potential action items for his loving Father to accomplish.

Prayer, simply put, is "talking to God." The sisters' telegram to Jesus was therefore a prayer of intercession. The sisters could have refused to send the telegram because of a belief that Jesus was too far away, or too busy elsewhere, to get involved. Those who refuse to pray for this reason were later termed "Deists" because of a belief that God was an absentee landlord too busy elsewhere to care about the situation in the slums of his creation. But the sisters knew Jesus did care and the telegram would be received. The sisters dared to join the "intercessory prayer team" that has been the critical tool of the praying life for God's people since at least the time of Abraham.[13] In the ongoing work of the kingdom of God, "nothing is more important than intercessory prayer."[14] To boldly "intercede" in prayer means to "go between, plead for another, represents the needs of one to another." In doing so, the center of attention was taken off of self and placed upon the needs of others. This is a self-giving type of prayer—and hard work.

Rather than bringing new unknown concerns to God, those who practice intercession sense in doing so that they are more "joining with" God in his ongoing concerns. God held Lazarus and the sisters in his longing gaze long before anyone else knew to do so. He was aware of the human situation and had already begun to respond. It was God who even prompted the sisters to send the telegram, waking them out of their preoccupation with caregiving and the total-absorption of a crisis. For it is of God the psalmist wrote, "He who watches over Israel will neither slumber nor sleep."[15] In sending the message to Jesus, the sisters were not only sending word to the one on earth most capable of helping, but also to the same one most capable of interceding to his Father on their behalf. For in taking their concerns to Jesus through intercession, the sisters were interceding to the "great interceder," who now sits "at the right hand of God, and is also interceding for us."[16] Jesus was Israel's true high priest, who "always lives to intercede for them."[17] Mary and Martha sent their telegram to Jesus that in "Jesus' name" it might become top priority in heaven.

Even more, their simple telegram showed the dogged persistence of two determined sisters. Regardless of physical circumstances, these sisters were unrelenting in getting a message to Jesus. The sisters were not certain where Jesus was located, what he was doing, or what other pressing matters might be on his plate. They did not care, because urgency and desperation made them bold. Jesus had taught his disciples to pray with this dogged determinism through several of his parables. A neighbor came calling for a loan of bread to provide a midnight snack for unexpected houseguests. The other neighbor, cozy in his bed, refused to get up to fetch the bread the other so urgently needed—until the persistence of the perpetual knock on the door eventually won the day and the needed bread was provided.[18] Later, a helpless widow refused to embrace her helplessness and instead stood up day after day to an unjust judge until her persistence won the day.[19] In each case, Jesus announced that his Father rewards persistence. His followers are to keep on seeking, keep on asking, keep on knocking until prayers are eventually rewarded. The early church called this form of intercession "supplication." It means to ask with earnestness, with intensity, and with perseverance. It announces to God and others how deadly serious Jesus-followers are about this thing called prayer.

The sisters also learned the secret of praying as they could, not as they could not. There was no time for the creativity of a poem or the sensitivity of a haiku. This was not the time for a novel or an editorial either. The sisters could only speak to Jesus with the simple words coming from their hearts, in the midst of a family crisis. Martha, as a high achiever, could not wait until she could craft the perfect message. Nor could she wait to send it until the kitchen was clean, the laundry done, and the day's chores all checked off the to-do list. Mary couldn't wait for that warm feeling to emerge from deep within that provided her artistic inspiration. The two sisters just needed to stop, think for a moment, and then make a petition to Jesus. The only bad telegram would be the one never written—just like the only bad prayers are the ones left unoffered. The sisters here learned the secret of praying out of the desperation found within them—not what *ought* to be in them. Theirs was a deep and requisite love, and that love was a call to pray.

God likes the correspondence. Even Jesus liked receiving telegrams. He wanted to be communicated with and liked knowing what was going on—even though he was omniscient. Parents love to be asked by children for what they already know the child will need; it deepens the relationship. A Christian monk named Theophan the Recluse once said it this way:

> Prayer is the test of everything; prayer is also the source of everything; prayer is the driving force of everything, prayer is also the director of everything. If prayer is right, everything is right. For prayer will not allow anything to go wrong.[20]

And so through praying one discovers that prayer is an act of love, telling God what he already knows—asking God to absorb our pain and also give what he longs to give.

And through the petitionary prayer of a simple telegram, Mary and Martha began to change. Prayer changes things—but especially people. Prayer is God's way of transforming and reshaping us. Those unwilling to change soon abandon prayer as a noticeable characteristic of life. Those who present their requests faithfully and persistently to God discover the greatest change comes deep within themselves. The apostle Paul explains it this way:

> Do not be anxious about anything, but in everything, by prayer and supplication, with thanksgiving, present your requests to God. And the peace of God, which transcends all understanding, will guard your hearts and minds in Christ Jesus. (Phil 4:6–7)

Mary and Martha sent Jesus a telegram, a petition of prayer, and everything changed. What they sent was faith seeking hope. The immediate result was a peace beyond understanding.

KONTAKION ON THE RAISING OF LAZARUS

Together sustained by faith, the two
    Announced to Christ and God the death
Of their brother, saying, "Hasten, come, Thou
    Who art always present in all places,
For Lazarus whom Thou dost love is ill: If
    Thou come near,
Death will vanish, and Thy friend will be
    Saved from corruption,
And the Jews will see that Thou, the Merciful
    One, has taken pity on
The tears of Mary and Martha."

—Romanus Melodus (490–556)[21]

When he heard this, Jesus said, "This sickness will not end in death. No, it is for God's glory so that God's Son may be glorified through it."

—JOHN 11:4

CHAPTER THREE

Disappointment with God
—or with Jesus, Anyway

O my God, deep calls unto deep. The deep of my profound misery calls to the deep of your infinite mercy.

—BERNARD OF CLAIRVAUX

You can do more than pray after you have prayed, but you cannot do more than pray until you have prayed. . . . Prayer is striking the winning blow; service is gathering up the results.

—S. D. GORDON

THE MESSENGER LEFT BETHANY with strict orders from Martha:

> Go find Jesus; he's somewhere near the Jordan River; I believe near the Dead Sea. Don't stop searching until you find him. When you do find him, give him this note—and don't give this telegram to anyone else. One of the apostles will try and take the note for you to Jesus, but you must insist! Place it in his hands, ask him to read it—and respond. Bring his response directly back to me. Is this clear?

The trusted servant on his valiant steed began making his way across Judea at breakneck speed. He arrived just as Jesus was wrapping up his daylong message at the river's edge. Jesus was surrounded by a mass of humanity each wanting a minute of his time: a blessing, a healing, a religious question answered. But when the messenger drew near, he clearly came with purpose. His boldness and resolve even interrupted Jesus in mid-sentence saying, "Jesus, I have an urgent message for you . . .from Bethany!"

"Bethany," Jesus replied, "I know who that's from. Come close." The line of questioners parted like the Red Sea as the messenger stepped forward. All those surrounding Jesus wondered if they would get a hint of the urgent situation facing the rabbi. As the messenger drew closer Jesus asked, "What does it say? Read it aloud." Everyone within earshot grew quiet with wonder. But the messenger didn't need to read it aloud—he had it memorized and knew every word by heart. Martha knew Jesus well and suspected Jesus might ask it be read aloud—he had no secrets. So Martha coached the messenger before he left to speak with urgency and compassion. They had gone over the exact words time and again before Martha ever let him go. "Say those words just right to get the message across," she said, coaching him beyond what anyone else had ever made the messenger do. The messenger then announced it just as he had rehearsed, saying,

Jesus, the friend you love is sick. Signed, Martha and Mary.

The apostles listening in knew the impact those words would have upon the heartstrings of Jesus. They knew there was no one short of his mother whom Jesus loved more than Lazarus. The sisters had used the Greek word *philein,* "the love of a friend," to describe the bond between Jesus and Lazarus. The sisters were telling Jesus that his best friend was very sick and things were critical. The one Jesus loved to go on long walks with couldn't walk. The one Jesus loved to laugh with could barely breathe. The one with whom Jesus shared a late-night conversation around the fire was burning up with fever.

Everyone within hearing distance wondered what Jesus would do. Was this going to be the end of the teaching sessions? Would the apostles start packing things up to break camp? Was Jesus going to get up and leave immediately—and by himself? Mary and Martha surely thought he would. They were convinced (as were the apostles) that the moment Jesus knew something was wrong with Lazarus, he'd make a beeline to Bethany to take care of it. That's what friends do, isn't it? The sisters knew Jesus was not one who loves, then abandons. But they also knew Jesus didn't always do what others expected of him. Even his own mother had to twist his arm to bring wine from water. Jesus listened for a "Go" only from his Father, and nothing else swayed him—at all. Jesus once explained, "I tell you the truth, the Son can do nothing by himself; he can do only what he sees his Father doing, because whatever the Father does the Son also does."[22] Jesus' ears were tuned to One Voice, and this meant he had eliminated the background noise of everything else.

But Jesus had clearly heard and understood the magnitude of the messenger's words concerning the one he loved. He knew from the force of the message, and the urgency of the messenger, that the sickness was serious. Martha wasn't the type of woman to overreact, and she would never call out to Jesus unless every kitchen recipe and every home remedy had been exhausted. What would Jesus do about this urgent and important message? What would his Father tell him? Jesus paused and listened for that still small voice. He pondered an inner prompting for just a moment. Then he replied to the messenger with the seriousness and firm conviction of a great physician making a critical diagnosis. He answered:

> Send this message back to the sisters, "This illness will not result in death. But it will result in the glory of God. God's Son will be glorified by it."

And with that the messenger took off, racing back to give the word to Mary and Martha. It sure sounded like good news! Great news even. . . . The messenger hurried back to share the sure and certain outcome Jesus promised with the sisters awaiting reply. How beautiful are the feet of those who bring good news!

Meanwhile, Mary and Martha were at home doing all they could, with what they had, to bring comfort and relief to their dear brother. Isn't that what good sisters, Jesus' adopted family, should do? Those wired like Mary make it their main task to bless and lift the spirits of a brother. But all the while Mary was still wondering, "When is Jesus going to get here?" She knew when the messenger left, how long a journey it would be, and how long it would take a motivated friend to return. "If my calculations are correct," she thought, "then Jesus should arrive here by two o'clock tomorrow—I sure hope Lazarus can hang on that long!"

When Mary finally shared her calculations with Martha, the logical and accountant-like Martha replied, "That's not realistic!" Mary was a "best case scenario" type of person, but Martha brought her back down to earth. So together they tried to figure out the exact time Jesus would return (a task many others have attempted over the last two millennia with similar results). Nevertheless, as all of this figuring, caregiving, praying, and pondering was going on there was one phrase they constantly repeated that brought great comfort: "When Jesus gets here, everything will be okay." Of this they were certain. They could think of no time Jesus had ever been present when things didn't turn out right. Simply put, Jesus made things "the way they were supposed to be."

But Lazarus's breathing soon grew weaker, and the doctor was called back to his bedside. The physician warned the sisters that Lazarus could be slipping away soon. But the two women, with their hope still in Jesus, simply replied, "When Jesus gets here, everything will be okay." Soon afterward, the local rabbi arrived to pray last rights over Lazarus as a faithful synagogue member now at death's door. Yet the sisters were still adamant in their belief, "When Jesus gets here everything will be okay." As Lazarus slipped in and out of consciousness even he still whispered through a strained voice, "Jesus?" And the sisters whispered their reply in his ear: "When Jesus gets here everything will be okay."

But Jesus didn't get there. Jesus wasn't allowed into the sick person's room. His Father had quarantined it off while placing Jesus in isolation—Jesus would not be allowed to enter.

Suddenly, Lazarus took a final turn. There was a gasp, a wheeze, and a choking sound. His heartbeat ceased, and he died. Lazarus was gone. The sisters' dear brother and Jesus' best friend was gone. The breath had left him, and his spirit had returned to God. The doctor present pulled the sheet over his head and recited a psalm: "How precious in the sight of the Lord is the death of his saints."[23] Within minutes the doctor led a crew of men from the village who took the dead body out of the house and began to make preparations for a swift burial. Mourners began to arrive. Mary and even Martha grew hysterical. And they grew numb. They never imagined a scenario where Jesus would not make it back to rescue the friend he loved so much. And Jesus never imagined a scenario where he would be placed in isolation and "sacred distancing" from the friend he loved so much.

Just what was Jesus doing that was so vitally important?

The sisters had a beef with Jesus. They too were Jesus' true friends. They had invested in a relationship with him. They had given freely of themselves, their resources, and their hearts. And as invested friends they felt they had a right to certain expectations of friendship—that Jesus would respond in kind back to them. Reciprocity demanded it. Now they were disappointed in Jesus, and also disappointed in God. They felt let down, betrayed, and abandoned. If friends don't let friends drink and drive a camel, how could a friend sit back and let his best friend just die? While doing nothing? The sisters found themselves numbered among the roll call of the faithful who have waged a formal complaint against God—and his lack of timing. Abraham waited a quarter of a century for God to keep a promise. Joseph wondered why bad things kept happening when he did the right thing. Habakkuk questioned the fairness of God's punishments. Paul wondered aloud why his thorn in the flesh was not removed.

When it comes to honest disappointment with God, generally three questions emerge: "Is God Unfair?" "Is God silent?" and "Is God hidden?"[24] "Is God Unfair?" is the comparative question asked when rewards and happiness seem to be doled out capriciously by the Almighty. Some people openly deny God, yet live long and prosper. Others like Lazarus serve God wholeheartedly, yet suffer deeply and die prematurely from an unseen virus. Because life is clearly unfair, God, in this view, is unfair also.

"Is God Silent?" is the question asked in contemplating God's "No!" response. In great agony people pick up prayer and pour out their souls to the Almighty—perhaps for the first time ever—or at least in a long time. They are desperate for God or at least a word from their creator. Yet many feel their prayers never reach the ceiling or fall on heaven's deaf ears when they do get through. The Bible tells of a God who speaks, but for those most longing for a word they appear to receive none.

"Is God Hidden?" is the question that arises when an evidently all-powerful being chooses to go off the grid. If God showed up for Abraham, Moses, Elijah, and the rest—why is the God who is the same yesterday, today, and tomorrow so unwilling to show his face to those needing to see him most? It doesn't seem fair. It doesn't seem right. It is, quite frankly, disappointing. Where is he?

When the sisters were happy and life was joyous, an hour in the synagogue could soon turn into a season of gratitude and praise. The sisters knew to praise God for the good things; but what do they do when the bad times come? Do they lay their hardships on God too? May they lay the hard times on his plate, or does politeness force them to give God a pass on the tragedies?

In their swirling disappointment they felt as if the window of heaven had been slammed shut and bolted tight. All they received back from any conversing with God was silence. Why was Jesus so painfully absent at just the moment he was most needed? What had happened to their ever-present help in times of trouble? Where is God when life hurts? For the sisters, at this moment, Jesus appeared hidden and silent—and it all certainly seemed unfair and unkind.

The laughter and joy Jesus had brought so often to the sisters' home had been replaced by a despair and foreboding—a thick fog set upon the house. The sisters, so often bubbling with warmth and radiating with delightful pleasantries, were numb. They were worn out from long days of constant care and cried out as the tears had all been spent. A later writer who lost a young wife to cancer described this feeling as being "mildly drunk, or concussed."[25] It is as if a barrier had arisen between the sisters and the rest of the world—they could not take in what was happening around them. It all was an out-of-body experience now.

Why do bad things happen to good people like Lazarus? And where is God in the midst of the agony and the deep suffering? The problem of suffering and evil and the silence of God were staring the sisters smack in the face. Why had God allowed Lazarus to suffer so intensely—and what purpose could it have possibly served? Why did death take their brother so soon when he was such a good man and so many lesser men lived on to a ripe old age? Mary and Martha were experiencing a disappointment with God based upon a universal problem with pain:

> If God were good, He would wish to make his creatures perfectly happy, and if God were almighty, he would be able to do what he wished. But the creatures are not happy. Therefore, God lacks either goodness, or power, or both. This is the problem of pain, in its simplest form.[26]

It's during this disappointment with God that many faulty answers have been tried and found wanting—answers that do not answer. Atheism denies the existence of God altogether, but that answer still leaves the sisters alone and in just as much pain. Polytheism offers the sisters a pantheon of gods in place of the One, but where among the options would the sisters turn in times of trouble? Science offers a naturalistic God of cause and effect who works through doctors and medicine—but the physicians had no vaccine that would bring back Lazarus. Pantheism offers a god too consumed with other things to engage in the human condition—here Mary and Martha are left on their own. Deism offers a god too distant to care. A demythologized God does indeed care, but is too weak to do anything about it. And the most modern of all responses to the question of suffering is to merely avoid the question while looking for a myriad of means to avoid the pain altogether.

Knowing there is no better answer than the Hebrew God provides, and still believing Jesus to be God's Messiah, the sisters were forced to deal with their disappointment in the same way as the prophets who came before them. Certainly, they were disappointed. And yes, they had big questions about what God was doing. But the sisters recognized that the person of faith frames her questions about God with the truths she knows to be certain about the nature of God. While they still questioned what God was doing and were dismayed at his silence, the sisters still chose to believe in a Faithful, Loving, and Good God. The prophet Habakkuk's disappointment with God came as he watched Israel suffer savagely at the hands of an evil empire. As he wrestled with what kind of God might do such a thing, he heard a voice remind, "The Lord is in his Holy Temple, let all the earth keep silent before him."[27] And so Habakkuk remembered the fame of his mighty God and again stood in awe of his deeds. He closed his brief letter, chock-full with disappointment in God, with these famous words:

> Though the fig tree does not bud and there are no grapes on the vines, though the olive crop fails and the fields produce no food, though there are no sheep in the pen and no cattle in the stalls, yet I will rejoice in the Lord, I will be joyful in God my Savior. (Hab 3:17–18)

A few years later the prophet Jeremiah would watch as Jerusalem was besieged. He looked on in wonder from the Mount of Olives as the walls of his beloved city were torn down. The beautiful gates were set ablaze and the temple ransacked. With the temple set on fire and the holy relics of God taken into captivity, Jeremiah navigated a bitter disappointment in God. Deep questions as to what God was doing followed. Yet in the midst of the questioning and disappointment, God gave Jeremiah these words to share with all Israel:

> I well remember the affliction and the wandering, and my soul is downcast within me. Yet this I call to mind and therefore I have hope: The steadfast love of the Lord never ceases, his mercies never come to an end. They are new every morning; great is your faithfulness. So I say to myself, "The Lord is all I need; therefore I will hope in him." (Lam 3:20–24)

In their disappointment, there was nothing else for the sisters to do but frame their doubts and disappointments in what they still knew to be true about God and about his Son, their friend Jesus. God was still Holy, Faithful, Loving, and Good—and so was, they had to believe, Jesus.

But still they were disappointed—quite so.

THE BUSTLE IN A HOUSE

> The bustle in a house
> The morning after death
> Is solemnest of industries
> Enacted upon earth, —
>
> The sweeping up the heart,
> And putting love away
> We shall not want to use again
> Until eternity.
>
> —Emily Dickinson (1830–1886)[28]

Now Jesus loved Martha and her sister and Lazarus. [6] So when he heard that Lazarus was sick, he stayed where he was two more days.

—JOHN 11:5–6

CHAPTER FOUR

Absence and Isolation

He allows the realm of darkness to seize his friend, drag him down to the underworld, and take possession of him. He acts like this so that human hope may perish entirely and human despair reach its lowest depths.

—PETER CHRYSOLOGUS

As we become aware of his absence we discover his presence, and as we realize that he left us we also come to know that he did not leave us alone.

—HENRY NOUWEN

THE MODERN IDEA OF "love" needs to be corrected.

When Martha and Mary sent their telegram to Jesus, the carefully chosen words included, "The friend you love (with a deep friendship love) is sick." But the Gospel writer tells us Jesus had a love for Lazarus (and for his sisters as well) that far surpassed the "friendship love" of which Martha and Mary wrote. The author states it this way, "Now Jesus loved [in Greek *agapan*, meaning with 'a complete and self-sacrificing love'] Martha and her sister and Lazarus." The author makes it clear there was no higher or deeper love, no greater affection, and no more surpassing tenderness than the love Jesus felt for his adopted family in Bethany. But then the author goes on to add a surprise, a shock really, with his next sentence: "Yet, when Jesus heard that Lazarus was sick, he stayed where he was two more days."[29]

Perhaps only the author John would use the Greek word "yet" (*os*) to take two things seemingly contradictory—Jesus' love for Lazarus and Jesus' staying behind—and add them together to get a sum that is true. John places both in suspension, love and absence, yet claims they arrive at truth and love. Somehow Jesus could love the sisters and his friend Lazarus as completely as any love the world had known, "yet" stay put and not go to them. The love of Christ generally compels one to "go," but here it compelled Jesus to "stay" put.

What was Jesus doing those two days that was so all-surpassingly important? What great deed kept him from hightailing it back to Bethany to be with Lazarus? What life-altering message did Jesus deliver then?

Nada. Nothing.

At least nothing of note to call special. Jesus camped near the Jordan and crowds came streaming out to listen to him from every countryside, village and hamlet. He spoke of repentance and getting one's heart right, of a new kingdom and a new kind of king. He legitimated his message and authenticated his king-worthiness with wonder-working power. The masses were coming and unburdening hearts, confessing sin, and finding release from the bondage unconfessed sin had bound them with for years. A new kind of kingdom, and a gospel justice towards the marginalized, was being proclaimed. And the transforming power of the Holy Spirit was unleashed—making broken lives whole again. For the next two days, Jesus continued on at the edge of the River Jordan to preach and to teach. It was as if Jesus hadn't a care in the world.

The text gives us no record of any special miracle he did during those two days. No record of any great teaching he proclaimed made its way into the annals of the New Testament. No record of any significant encounter with someone arises from those dates. For Jesus, it was just two more routine days. Yes, it was noteworthy because it was two days of Jesus' roughly one thousand he spent over three short years of ministry. But what happened those two days was "par for the course" when it came to Jesus' daily activities. And that being so, one could wonder, as the apostles probably did, why Jesus kept going through his same old routine when the ones in Bethany were going through such an agonizing and painful experience. Why did he choose to self-isolate and stay in place living out the "same ole, same ole" when Lazarus lay dying and Martha and Mary knelt pleading for his return?

Because John's Gospel grants insider information, readers have known since the prologue that Jesus was fully God, and likewise fully man. That said, Jesus as "fully God" knew exactly what was happening back in Bethany. He had omniscience ("all-knowing power") and understood precisely what his friends were going through. While residing at the Jordan, Jesus' spiritual eyes, once on the sparrow, were now watching over Lazarus and the family from afar. Jesus absorbed every cry of abandonment as the sisters questioned God and wondered aloud, "Where could Jesus possibly be?" He knew the sisters and Lazarus himself were puzzled beyond belief when he failed to show as he could. He internalized their disappointment with God, and also with him.

As the Great Physician, Jesus knew the composition of the virus that attacked Lazarus. He knew Lazarus was sick to the point of death; he felt each gasp for breath, every labored word, each agonizing sound. Jesus even knew the precise moment when the illness exacted the last ounce of life and Lazarus died. Perhaps Jesus even absorbed that pain in some physical way in the midst of the day's routine, writhing in a quick burst of anguish before returning to the labors at hand. Jesus heard from afar the sisters' mournful cries as they wailed uncontrollably at unthinkable loss. Jesus knew the town was coming out to join in the grieving, and he knew that in a matter of moments, a messenger would arrive with a message of hope for the sisters *from him* in the midst of their despair. Jesus knew the messenger would soon say:

> This illness will not result in death. But it will result in the glory of God. God's Son will be glorified through it.
> —Jesus

When it was read aloud for all in the house to hear, Jesus absorbed the mocking insults from visitors—and the anger of sisters now dealing with that stage of their grief. The family's longtime friends, who had met and knew Jesus, wondered aloud, "How could Jesus be so wrong? And why would he abandon his friends at a time like this?" Yet Jesus stayed where he was and kept on teaching for two more days.

Humanity can identify with the human side of Jesus in this moment; most all have been there. There are moments in the recent past, and more to come in the future, when God forces his children to take a seat in the waiting room. Each is called to self-isolation and an internal quarantine undesired and unwanted. It is the seat taken when there is nothing one can do in a pandemic or other current crisis, yet it's all anyone can think about.

In the waiting of life room (like with COVID-19 in 2020) there's a cosmic drama going on that demands all of one's attention, all of one's heart, all of one's aspirations, all of the hope for good news . . . but yet there's nothing anyone can really do physically to alter the outcome. Hands have been tied, masks have been put on, and social distancing has been strictly enforced.

Been there?

Certainly. Isolation is the waiting room that has a seat with every person's name. Each person longs to do something about the crisis and to be a part of the solution. But all that can be accomplished by most but a few health professionals are the routine tasks of every day. What would normally be called "work" is now simply a diversion, a distraction from the real focus of the day. Most try to make the best of the routine while the heart is far away with loved ones elsewhere. In every emergency room (if guests are even allowed admittance) and in any waiting room, concerned friends thumb through magazines, or they flip open laptops opting for some routine work. They might even try to get their income tax in order. Anything that can be done to wish away the hours while waiting for life and death news would be welcomed. Jesus stayed in routine, did his job, and waited for his Father to give him marching orders. But he was working from a seat in the self-isolation of the waiting room.

Jesus stayed away those two more days because he only acted on God's timing—and no one else's. But an even fuller explanation is found in Jesus who, fully man and fully God, "needed to learn obedience through the things that he suffered."[30] At a deeper level, God the Father was instructing God his Son. School was in session for Jesus, and there was a lesson from the Father that Jesus had to learn and absorb. Interestingly, the God-man Jesus was limited by time and space like all the rest of God's creatures. Jesus was bound to a body just like the rest of humanity. Only by "going through" the ordeal of isolation could "experience be the teacher" now even for Jesus. Like the rest of creation, Jesus had to "grow through what he was going through." Some lessons are learned no other way. At this point in the story God, the loving Father, took Jesus his Son and placed him in the waiting room and might have said,

> You can't leave yet. You may want to go, you may want to help, but for the next two days you're going to sit here in isolation and you're going to absorb the pain and the grief from afar—feel what it's like to live in the waiting room. As Abraham once tied the hands of his son Isaac, now I am tying yours.

Social distancing was really the Father's "sacred distancing." Lessons were being learned from a distance that could not be learned in close proximity. It was the distance that added the divine to the event.

And so, Jesus sat.

And he waited.

And he absorbed what he could learn no other way.

Those with a worshipful heart are often deeply formed by waiting. David proclaimed in psalm after psalm a thanksgiving learned in self-isolation and spiritual quarantine. He writes, "I waited patiently for the Lord; he turned to me and heard my cry" and "Wait for the Lord; be strong and take heart and wait for the Lord."[31] David discovered his soul cried to the Lord in the self-isolation in a unique and powerful way—"I wait for the Lord, my soul waits, and in his word I put my hope. My soul waits for the Lord more than watchmen wait for the morning"[32]—and in this waiting a longing and thirst for God was heightened.

The prophet Isaiah also discovered a blessing associated with isolation, "The Lord longs to be gracious to you; he rises to show you compassion. For the Lord is a God of justice. Blessed are all who wait for him!"[33] Later Isaiah pronounces that in the sacred distancing, God gives newfound strength to the weary:

> Even youths grow tired and weary, and young men stumble and fall; but those who wait in the Lord will renew their strength. They will soar on wings like eagles, they will run and not grow weary, they will walk and not be faint. (Isa 40:30–31)

Waiting for good news, waiting for adoption; waiting for a blessed hope—the Bible is rich with good things that come to those who wait.

But viewing Jesus sitting in self-isolation and spiritual quarantine is a different story. It seems odd that the one who so often stepped forward to heal and bless now plops himself down with his hands tied. John allows his readers to go sit with Jesus. They get to watch him, experience his pathos, and learn from his stillness. And what lessons are learned from him in the isolation? First and foremost, Jesus demonstrates that no human is in control of life—only God the Father has his hand on the controls. That lesson is learned quickly in the self-isolation and social distancing of a pandemic, as if a neon sign stated, "You are not in control here!" The self-quarantine also magnifies how important people are to life; work is a diversion but people and relationships are the real thing. And Zoom may be nice, but the WiFi from the Jordan River didn't allow for even that lesser contact.

The meaning of trust is learned sitting in isolation, whether it be two days at the Jordan or fourteen days in a bedroom. The self-isolation is God's laboratory to experience dependence upon him. The lab work forces everyone to "lift up eyes to the hills of heaven from whence our help will come."[34] Those in the waiting room of self-quarantine discover what it means to "wait on the Lord to renew their strength" and receive an energy to continue unwearied by the challenges thrust upon them. And perhaps most painful of all, self-isolation brings the realization that the ways of God are sometimes far different than expected. Especially in matters of life and death.

So why does God put his loved ones where all they can do is live in isolation and wait things out? Why does God allow COVID-19 to disrupt our world, kill our elderly and compromised, empty our calendars, and wreak havoc on our economy? Some carry coronavirus with no seeming effect at all, others need a ventilator to spare them from certain death. Some get to keep working, others must shut down for the good of society. What is the lesson learned in these moments? Why has God put so many in self-isolation and personal quarantine? And what is it that each is supposed to learn there?

Entering inside a spiritual season of quarantine, those placed there discover isolation is often a part of the cure—even a vital part. God places his loved ones there to grow through what is gone through and to learn a deeper obedience through the suffering absorbed. Even at the dawn of creation there was no daylight until after there was dawn—why would waiting and isolation be any different?[35] There is no joy in the morning until there are tears shed in beds at night. There is no hope of resurrection until a death and a burial—only after a season of deep mourning. Only then may joy come.

Self-isolation reminds all of the truth of the farmer: the premise of sowing and reaping. Waiting and isolation must be sown in tears, that joy may be harvested after. Why was Jesus quarantined there at the Jordan? Remember in Hebrews 5:8 it tells that Jesus, although he was a son, learned obedience by the things that he suffered. And only when he had been perfected by these things could he then grant eternal life to all those who obeyed him. Some things can only be understood when tested by fire, when placed in a crucible moment. In the crucible like that of a global pandemic, the testing by fire forces an experience of desperation in those now wholly dependent upon God.

There in self-isolation we understand why David could sound almost like an atheist: "My God, my God, why have you forsaken me?" If ever one sits in quarantine, desperately pleading for an answer that doesn't come, it's then that David's inquisition of God makes sense. Waiting long enough will drive most anyone to say, "God, what are you doing? God, why is this happening? God, where are you? My God, my God, why have you forsaken me?"

Some sit in the cell of spiritual isolation right now, today. If so, they soon will realize God has placed them there for a reason—for his purposes. Everyone will grow through this—God guarantees it. For all going through a hard time, it will make them stronger—more fit for the kingdom to come. While sitting in quarantine, we have time to focus upon what Jesus did while sitting in his own. Jesus' example encourages each in waiting to look around the isolated community and see who else is sitting there as well. Jesus used his two-day wait to "be Jesus to the people where he was" by focusing upon them, their needs, their challenges, their stories, their pains, their heartaches. Even as he held special concern for the care and comfort of one specific family far away, he did not miss the opportunity to also be the hands, eyes, feet, and mouth of God to those all around him.

When Jesus met a woman with an issue of blood, he asked her to tell him her story—then he listened intently to hear of God's work within her life. When children were around, he invited them close, bounced them on his knee, laughed with them, blessed them. When helpless poor mothers came asking for mercy, Jesus gave them his time even when the culture told him not to do so. Jesus started his ministry announcing he would focus upon bringing "good news to the poor, recovery of sight to the blind, release to those in bondage and today as a day of God's favor to all people"—and nowhere better to do such things than in a waiting room, a group of ten or less, or whatever the situation demands.

As Jesus learned life lessons from the experiences in his isolation, so all who follow him will learn as well in their own. Look at Jesus and learn from him. As amazing and mysterious as it might sound, it's possible that even the Almighty over all creation watched Jesus in his quarantine and isolation to learn some lessons that might help him a few weeks later as well. Imagine that.

And so the words Jesus sent to Mary and Martha become the words for all who follow Jesus into self-isolation or spiritual quarantine. There is nothing else. And it's these words that give us hope:

Whatever situation you're in, whatever you're going through, this situation will not end in defeat. It won't. It will result in the glory of God. The Son of God will be glorified through you and through what you're going through.

God places children he loves in seasons of isolation for a reason. And while there, he wants them to look to the right, and to the left, and to understand that he sits there with all who enter that sacred space as well. It is faith, and the faith of the family and friends that share in the challenge being faced, that is being tested—refined by the fire.

Before making a beautiful piece of jewelry, silversmiths take the silver and place it in a smelting pot. They hold it over an intensely hot fire. It is the skill of the silversmith that carefully watches over the processing of the silver. He wants to make sure the temperature is just right—hot but not too hot. The heat is raised just enough so that the impurities in the silver are dislodged but not so hot as to injure, and ruin, the silver. Likewise, if found in spiritual isolation today, all must understand that God has the heat up, but not too high. He's purifying the precious ones he loves. He's making all things whole, returning them to their purest form. The heat may seem to be more than anyone can possibly bear, but God as the expert silversmith will not let it injure his children.

How does the silversmith know when the silver is ready? It's really quite simple. He knows it's ready when he can see his image in the silver. A silversmith content with silver filled with impurities would be less than a craftsman. For God to be content with less than godly character in us would make him less than loving. The impurities and stains must come out so that the brilliance and luster of that which is precious may be revealed. God will do whatever it takes to purify and to strengthen his children—his goal is to see his image in each one. God already loves all, and now his work, and the waiting in isolation, is to make his children more lovable.

THIRST

The nurse said, your father really looks at you
when you walk into the room—

he stares at you,
she said, he must have something to tell you.

But he never tells you.

Later, another hospice worker listened to this story.
She said, no, you know,

sometimes, as we're leaving this world,
our world contracts to the small space of the room,

to the few things we love.

Your father wasn't looking at you because he had
something to tell you, no,

he was looking at you because he loved you, she said.
It was near the end, she said,

he was drinking you in.

   —Ed Madden (b. 1963)[36]

"And then he (Jesus) said to his disciples, "Let us go back to Judea." ⁸ "But Rabbi," they said, "a short while ago the Jews there tried to stone you, and yet you are going back?"

⁹ Jesus answered, "Are there not twelve hours of daylight? Anyone who walks in the daytime will not stumble, for they see by this world's light. ¹⁰ It is when a person walks at night that they stumble, for they have no light."

¹¹ After he had said this, he went on to tell them, "Our friend Lazarus has fallen asleep; but I am going there to wake him up." ¹² His disciples replied, "Lord, if he sleeps, he will get better." ¹³ Jesus had been speaking of his death, but his disciples thought he meant natural sleep.

¹⁴ So then he told them plainly, "Lazarus is dead, ¹⁵ and for your sake I am glad I was not there, so that you may believe. But let us go to him." ¹⁶ Then Thomas (also known as Didymus) said to the rest of the disciples, "Let us also go, that we may die with him."

—JOHN 11:7-16

CHAPTER FIVE

Falling Asleep

To come to the pleasure you have not, you must go
by a way in which you enjoy not.

—SAINT JOHN OF THE CROSS

Listen, I tell you a mystery: We will not all sleep, but we will all be changed—in
a flash, in the twinkling of an eye, at the last trumpet. For the trumpet will
sound, the dead will be raised imperishable, and we will be changed.

—1 COR 15:51–52

JESUS SAT QUARANTINED BY Almighty God.

In isolation he absorbed all God wanted him to learn.

And he went through his routine.

Our text then explains that after two long days, it was time. Time for
him to go. Like a general with fresh commands, Jesus went to his apostles
and announced their new marching orders: "Today it's time for us to go
back to Judea." In unison the apostles let out a tremendous groan. Thomas
blurted out, "Oh, no. Not Judea. Not there again. Last time they nearly
stoned you to death!" Being stoned was no mere rock fight. Stoning meant
being seized and dragged from the city, thrust into a pit, and having large
stones heaved upon your body, cracking ribs and crushing skulls. It was no

place for a diplomatic leader like Jesus to go again, and Thomas was acting as bodyguard in deeming it a "no-fly zone" for his leader.

Jesus was saying "Judea" because it was the region of land (from which the word "Jew" gets its name) in southern Israel containing within its boundaries Lazarus's city of Bethany. Jesus wanted to go back to Bethany, but the disciples knew that two miles from Bethany, and within the same region, was Jerusalem. And the last two times they'd been back to Jerusalem, guess what had happened? Religious leaders had put a price on Jesus' head as a blasphemer worthy of death. It was just a short time ago that he was standing in the temple stating, "I and the Father are one," and everyone was grabbing stones ready to kill him. Now Jesus was saying, "Hey guys, I've got a great idea. Let's go back to Judea."

You do have to pardon the apostles for not sharing their master's death wish. But Jesus explained his unique perspective on the situation: "You know what? My Father has given me twelve hours of daylight, and they're not all spent. God's given me things to do. He's given me people to help. And while it's daylight and while there is still time, I'm going to do the things that God has bidden me to do. When night comes, that's when people stumble and fall because there is no more light." Jesus' own "night" would soon come,[37] when Judas began the betrayal process. But until then, it was daylight, and God's servant must use the day ahead to bring glory to the Father.

John begins his gospel introducing us to Jesus as the preexistent "Word" (the *Logos*) who is the light and life for the whole world. Throughout John's Prologue the words "light" and "life" take center stage, as a life truly lived involves living in the revealed light of God—shown through the person of Jesus. Later, Jesus in his Sermon on the Mount would charge his followers, "You are the light of the world; a city set on a hill that cannot be hidden. . . . Let your light shine before men that they may see your good deeds and praise your Father in heaven."[38] Even later, in the temple Jesus would cry out in a loud voice, "I am the light of the world. Whoever follows me will never walk in darkness, but have the light of life."[39] Jesus was now going back to Judea because the light of God was leading him there, much as it had led the three wise men to his manger years ago. And Jesus invited his disciples to join him in the light. "We're going there because our friend Lazarus is asleep," Jesus explained, "and I need to wake him up."

Now, when the disciples heard that Lazarus was resting comfortably in sleep, they latched onto his condition as their extraction strategy. "Asleep?"

they asked, "Lazarus is asleep, and you want us to go and wake him up? People who are asleep, they get well. Sleeping is the best thing you can do for your health. If you're sleeping, you're going to get better." The disciples were confident that Jesus' services (and their own) would not be needed. Nature's own home remedy would do the trick; sleep it off and wake up feeling better.

Their response was the kind of thing many people say when confronted with a scenario that could cost them life, limb, or property. Easy reductionism. They figure out the quickest way to dismiss this situation, and they show Jesus his "out" by which to not get involved. "If people don't have a job, its probably their fault." They don't need your assistance. "If people caught the coronavirus, they were probably irresponsible." They don't need your caring concern. "If elderly in quarantine have no one to shop for them, they must have raised lazy kids." They don't need your help. "If businesses had been frugal and cost-effective, they'd be fine." They don't need your support. The apostles wanted a world where people are responsible for the hand dealt them—and don't deserve anyone else's personal involvement to get better. To avoid getting involved in a messy situation, it's easier to reduce the challenge to a simplistic argument that allows easy dismissal and personal detachment. It's easy to say, "Not my problem." But that was the course the priest and the Levite took in Jesus' famous good Samaritan parable, and Jesus would have none of it. It was daylight. He was moving out. Lazarus needed to wake up.

After speaking to his disciples in metaphoric terms, Jesus cut through all their reductionist arguments with a few simple, yet painful, words: "Oh, no. We're going to Bethany. And we're going to Bethany because Lazarus is dead." There . . . he said it. His best friend was dead. Dead asleep. Sleeping in death. Saint Augustine would later write, "It was true that Lazarus was sleeping. To his sisters he was dead; to our Lord he was sleeping. To those who could not raise him again, he was dead."[40] But to the one who as Logos spoke the world into being and then rested on the seventh day, death was as sleep to him.

To awaken the dead was the stuff of the great dramas of the Greek theater. It was the longing of the great tragedies of Shakespeare, and the hope of Snow White and the other Disneyesque tales of childhood. For all others, awakening the dead was the stuff of legends and great epic tales, but for Jesus nothing of this life precluded him from awakening his friend again. Lazarus would, like every person who had died since Adam and Eve, be awakened again at the final day. But Jesus was going to Bethany to short-circuit that process and bring his friend back again—now.

"Falling asleep" as a phrase to speak of death did not originate with Jesus. "Sleep" is the imagery of Scripture from Job to Jesus to John. However, the image does take on added meaning among Jesus-followers from the time of Lazarus forward. Moses had spoken of "the sleep of death" as early as Psalm 90, and Daniel had prophesied, "Multitudes who sleep in the dust of the earth will awake: some to everlasting life and others to shame and everlasting contempt."[41] Jesus used the analogy of death as sleep earlier in his healing ministry. Remember the time he went to heal the daughter of Jairus and arrived just after the girl had died? Jesus entered the room of the dead girl and exclaimed, "Why all this wailing and commotion? The child is not dead but asleep." At that time people laughed, but Jesus had the last laugh.[42] Later, the earliest followers of Jesus used the phrase in their descriptions of death as well. After Stephen's defense in Acts 7, he was taken outside the city and stoned to death. As he lay dying, the text tells that he cried out, "Lord do not hold this sin against them," and then "he fell asleep." Later in Paul's preaching he references Kind David, "who fell asleep and was buried with his fathers and his body decayed."[43]

A few years after Jesus, Paul explained this concept of Christian death as a "falling asleep" most vividly in his first letters to the Thessalonians and Corinthians. In Paul's most famous passage about Christian death, he writes,

> Brothers and sisters, we do not want you to be uninformed about those who sleep in death, so that you do not grieve like the rest of mankind, who have no hope. For we believe that Jesus died and rose again, and so we believe that God will bring with Jesus those who have fallen asleep in him. According to the Lord's word, we tell you that we who are still alive, who are left until the coming of the Lord, will certainly not precede those who have fallen asleep. (1 Thess 4:13–15)

When Paul equates Christian death to sleep, he could mean a sort of "nap" believers take until Jesus comes again to wake them up. To the Christian who dies and has thus fallen asleep, the experience is basically as instantaneous as taking a nap and waking up. One might awaken a bit disoriented but can easily enter into the new reality of being awake again. Often, we have no idea how long we sleep, but awaken as if life has gone on uninterrupted by our slumber. Others find this "asleep" in death to be more like "lounging" on the beach or in a beautiful garden ("paradise" means a beautiful garden for rest).

Those who "sleep" in the Lord are in a state of restful happiness. N. T. Wright argues for a different view of the term "sleep" when he writes,

> Though this is sometimes described as sleep, we shouldn't take this to mean that it is a state of unconsciousness. Had Paul thought that, I very much doubt that he would have described life immediately after death as "being with Christ," which is far better. Rather, *sleep* here means that the *body* is "asleep" in the sense of "dead," while the real person—however we want to describe him or her—continues.[44]

Perhaps the term *hibernation* as a way of thinking about such sleep better serves the faith-filled. In that state of hibernation an animal moves in and out of consciousness while sleeping, resting, lounging, and awaiting a coming season when it will return to an earth renewed and ready to receive it.

No matter how exactly the faithful sleep in death, nor how long they sleep, or how they awaken, it must seem "instantaneous" to those asleep when Jesus bids them rise again. Interestingly, Paul finds no spiritual advantage for those who are awake when the Lord Jesus returns over those who have already died and fallen asleep. Those who "sleep" appear to receive a fast-pass (think Disneyworld) to the front of the line and meet the Lord first in line.

Later in Paul's great chapter on the resurrection, he makes his case for a new bodily life. This life comes in a new immortal and glorious body (on a new earth) after this life, and after death where one has fallen asleep. First in his core teaching about the tenets of the Christian faith he states,

> For what I received I passed on to you as of first importance: that Christ died for our sins according to the Scriptures, that he was buried, that he was raised on the third day according to the Scriptures, and that he appeared to Cephas, and then to the Twelve. After that, he appeared to more than five hundred of the brothers and sisters at the same time, most of whom are still living, though some have fallen asleep. (1 Cor 15:3–6)

Later in arguing about the vital nature of the resurrection to the truth of the Christian faith he states assuredly:

> For if the dead are not raised, then Christ has not been raised either. And if Christ has not been raised, your faith is futile; you are still in your sins. Then those also who have fallen asleep in Christ

are lost. If only for this life we have hope in Christ, we are of all people most to be pitied. But Christ has indeed been raised from the dead, the first-fruits of those who have fallen asleep. (1 Cor 15:16–20)

In each passage, Paul reminds the early church that death is not an ending of a relationship; the computer has not "crashed" and all memory been lost. Even more, death is not even a "powering off" of a life before being "restarted" by the Lord in a day to come. A computer in "sleep" mode looks to the eye as though it is "off" and lifeless—without power at all. Yet "sleep" mode in no way alters the memory, power, or functionality of the unit—it just means it is resting for a season until it is bumped back on again. Likewise, falling asleep does not alter the relationship with God, but does alter the immediate circumstances of the one sleeping. Lazarus had joined Moses and David and Daniel and all those who have fallen asleep in God while awaiting the moment when Christ would come to awaken them again.

In no way was Jesus making light of the pain, agony, and tragic consequences of death by calling it "sleep." No one who has lost a loved one in a pandemic could ever again trivialize death, and neither could Jesus. As a matter of fact, the only death he never called "sleep" was the death he would die for all mankind upon the cross. Jesus knew death was a painful and agonizing snuffing out of life—a ripping, the great divorce. Therefore, Jesus also viewed this somber moment with human eyes and from an earthly point of view. "Lazarus has died," Jesus explained. "His life is over, his life has ended."

Yet Jesus then added something more his disciples could not believe was coming out of his mouth. They had no category of friendship to understand how Jesus could utter such things about his closest friend. Jesus' followers knew how much he loved Lazarus, they knew the importance of Lazarus in his life, and so could hardly believe their ears when Jesus continued on,

Lazarus is dead, and I am glad for your sake that it has happened, that you might believe.

My best friend is gone. My soulmate is dead. The person I related to more closely than any other has passed away. And I'm glad for your sake that it happened. Now let's go to him.

Before Jesus could go, he had to stay. Before Jesus could serve, he had to sit. Before Jesus could respond, he had to rest. Before Jesus could support, he had to first absorb. Before Jesus could be savior, he had to be still. Jesus' waiting in isolation and quarantine gave full scope to death. Jesus gave free reign to the grave to do its horrid work, and allowed corruption to begin to have its way. Church father Peter Chrysologus goes further:

> Jesus prohibits neither putrefaction nor stench from taking their normal course. He allows the realm of darkness to seize his friend, drag him down to the underworld, and take possession of him. He acts like this so that human hope may perish entirely and human despair reach its lowest depths.[45]

Jesus waited for Lazarus to die, staying in place until he could tell his disciples with certainty that Lazarus was dead. Then he announced it, adding, "And I am glad." Glad that Mary and Martha were hurting in an unimaginable way? Of course not! Glad that Lazarus had been released from his pain and illness? Obviously. Glad Lazarus was in line for a new and glorious body? Certainly. But he specified the main reason he was glad: "For *your sake* I am glad I was not there, so that you may believe."[46] Because of Lazarus's death, the disciples were about to see sorrow become joy and mourning become dancing. Jesus was glad that resurrection would now be made manifest through his friend Lazarus. Jesus then invited his disciples to follow: "Come, let us go to him."

Thomas, most likely in Peter's absence,[47] then spoke on behalf of the full band of disciples: "Let's all go with him, that we may die alongside him." A German minister executed by Hitler, Dietrich Bonhoeffer, once noted,

> The cross is laid on every Christian. The first Christ-suffering which every man must experience is the call to abandon the attachments of this world. It is that dying of the old man which is the result of his encounter with Christ. As we embark upon discipleship, we surrender ourselves to Christ in union with His death—we give over our lives to death. Thus it begins; the cross is not the terrible end to an otherwise God-fearing and happy life, but it meets us at the beginning of our communion with Christ. When Christ calls a man, he bids him come and die.[48]

Thomas was first to understand this pathway to discipleship. Jesus calls Christ-followers to be witnesses, even martyrs,[49] subject to the call of the One who invites them to "come." Thomas's words place him on the positive side of the thin line separating martyrdom and suicide. Suicide is the expression of a stoic spirit resolved to giving up on life; martyrdom is the response of the warrior spirit resolved to stand alongside Jesus even to the bitterest of ends—and in so doing to discover life worth living. In Thomas (later somewhat undeservedly dubbed "Doubting Thomas") we find the words of supreme sacrifice and the definition of all discipleship: "taking up his cross to follow Jesus." Thomas's words become the mantra for those who decide to follow most closely after Jesus: "Let us go with him, that we may die alongside him as well."

QUEEN MAB

> How wonderful is Death,
> Death, and his brother Sleep!
> One, pale as yonder waning moon
> With lips of lurid blue;
> The other, rosy as the morn
> When throned on ocean's wave
> It blushes o'er the world;
> Yet both so passing wonderful!

> —Percy Bysshe Shelley (1792–1822)[50]

"On his arrival, Jesus found that Lazarus had already been in the tomb for four days. [18] Now Bethany was less than two miles from Jerusalem, [19] and many Jews had come to Martha and Mary to comfort them in the loss of their brother.[20] When Martha heard that Jesus was coming, she went out to meet him, but Mary stayed at home.

[21] "Lord," Martha said to Jesus, "if you had been here, my brother would not have died. [22] But I know that even now God will give you whatever you ask." [23] Jesus said to her, "Your brother will rise again." [24] Martha answered, "I know he will rise again in the resurrection at the last day."

[25] Jesus said to her, "I am the resurrection and the life. The one who believes in me will live, even though they die; [26] and whoever lives by believing in me will never die."

—JOHN 11:17–26A

Chapter Six

Confronting God

What do people mean when they say, "I am not afraid of God because I know He is good"? Have they never even been to a dentist?

—C. S. Lewis

A good name is better than fine perfume, and the day of death better than the day of birth. [2] It is better to go to a house of mourning than to go to a house of feasting, for death is the destiny of everyone; the living should take this to heart. [3] Frustration is better than laughter, because a sad face is good for the heart. [4] The heart of the wise is in the house of mourning but the heart of fools is in the house of pleasure.

—Eccl 7:1–4

Who gets invited to the funeral?

Solomon, the wisest of kings, counseled in Ecclesiastes that it's more important to go to a funeral than a dinner party. A house filled with grief is a more significant place to attend than a house of feasting—because death will be the destiny of all. Family and friends will attend the funeral for sure; it's practically required. Work associates and neighbors might drop something from a busy schedule to be present. An old friend of the family might be sought out to come and say a few words. That person will get a special invite—they might even fly her in from far away. When the funeral is your own, who are those invitees?

The answer to that question separates followers of Jesus from every other major world religion. If someone is Buddhist, no need to invite Buddha to attend the funeral; Buddha is dead. If they are Jewish, they won't invite Abraham, Moses, or Elijah to the funeral. Though Abraham may be the father of your people, Moses the great lawgiver, and Elijah the greatest of the prophets, they are each dead. If they are Muslim, they won't invite Mohammed to attend their funeral. He is buried at Mecca, and has not been seen or heard from in almost 1,500 years. But if someone is Christian, a true follower of Jesus, the one person they know to invite to the funeral is the Lord Jesus himself.

Some people are "wedding crashers," attending weddings without knowing anyone, merely for the food and drink. And come to think of it, Jesus did make a wedding pretty unforgettable once. While many people can strive to be the "life of the party," Jesus was equally the "life of the funeral." There is something about Jesus and funerals! Until the time of Jesus, death was the dark world of the evil one, Satan. Death was his dominion; hell, his party place. Satan led an assault upon life itself, and his trump card stated clearly, "Death wins!" Since the exit from the garden, death had won every time and twice on Sundays. But when Jesus started showing up at funerals, amazing, unbelievable, death-defying things happened regularly:

> Soon afterward, Jesus went to a town called Nain, and his disciples and a large crowd went along with him. As he approached the town gate, a dead person was being carried out—the only son of his mother, and she was a widow. And a large crowd from the town was with her. When the Lord saw her, his heart went out to her and he said, "Don't cry." Then he went up and touched the bier they were carrying him on, and the bearers stood still. He said, "Young man, I say to you, get up!" The dead man sat up and began to talk, and Jesus gave him back to his mother. (Luke 7:11–15)

> When he arrived at the house of Jairus, he did not let anyone go in with him except Peter, John and James, and the child's father and mother. Meanwhile, all the people were wailing and mourning for her. "Stop wailing," Jesus said. "She is not dead but asleep." They laughed at him, knowing that she was dead. But he took her by the hand and said, "My child, get up!" Her spirit returned, and at once she stood up. Then Jesus told them to give her something to

eat. Her parents were astonished, but he ordered them not to tell anyone what had happened. (Luke 8:51–56)

Whatever life and death matters folks were going through, and in whatever isolation they might be, at just the right time Jesus just might show up. If that happened, all bets were off.

For two long days at the Jordan River, Jesus had stayed where he was and continued to minister to the wants and needs of hundreds of hurting people. He did so because that was his anointed task[51]—given by his Father—that he was told to do as long as there was light to do it. His Father's actions spoke louder than words: "You stay put and go about your daily business, while all the while I know your heart will be in Bethany. Lazarus will die, and you will miss the funeral. Stay down there at the Jordan, meet with people and heal their hurts. I want you to know what it's like to help people even while your heart is far away where the one that you love is dying. I want you to stay put and I want you to isolate." Sit in quarantine while others gather for the funeral of your best friend. Sit while death comes knocking on Lazarus's door. Miss the funeral and the closure it affords. Absorb it all; take it all in.

Even Jesus needed to experience what it's like for things not to happen as one would like—to miss the significant event of a friend. Remember the writer of Hebrews explained, "Son though he was, Jesus learned obedience from what he suffered and, once made perfect, he became the source of eternal salvation for all who obey him."[52] Even Jesus, though fully God, could learn some things only through the tried and true method of personal experience. Jesus knows what it's like to be in isolation when others are gathering to mourn.

Jesus realized there was a funeral beginning to take shape for his best friend in the world. Jesus knew mourners were gathering and wailing. Jesus could feel the moaning and great sobs of tears flowing within the home where he had so often eaten, laughed, and loved. Jesus agonized over the fact that Mary and Martha were going through a difficult time and he was unable to attend. He also knew each sister would manage their grief differently. Martha would clean everything in sight, bury herself in preparing food, and offer hospitality to mourners gathering in a mostly fruitless attempt to comfort her. Mary, on the other hand, would be welcoming each new well-wisher with a smile amidst her tears. She would invite them to sit and tell her stories of Lazarus and the hidden exploits of a brother they realized had done so much they knew nothing about. Jesus knew both were grieving, each managing grief differently—yet both were silently frustrated with Jesus' own absence. And they were disappointed in God as well. Still, Jesus only took marching orders from his Father, and the Father had said, "Isolate and wait."

Finally, it was time for Jesus to leave the waiting room. It was as is if *Jehovah-Rophe*[53] (God as Surgeon General) came out the emergency room doors, entered the isolation room, and finally told Jesus, "You can end quarantine now and go see the patient." That is where we find Jesus when he announces, "Okay, it's time!" The disciples, of course, began in vain to talk Jesus out of it: "If Lazarus is sleeping then he will be fine!" But when they could not dissuade him, they followed anyway. In so doing, they learned the ways of God as they grew through what they journeyed through.

The journey to Bethany thus began. The Jesus caravan of tents, cooking materials, bedding, and traveling team (probably twenty or so people in all including Jesus, twelve apostles, women supporters and caregivers, and other travelers like Mattias and Barsabbas[54]) began the slow walk across the Judean desert, through the hill country, and towards Bethany. One is left to wonder what Jesus and his motley crew talked about along the way. The passage Jesus often recited at the synagogue informed his normal travel itinerary:

> Hear, O Israel: The Lord our God, the Lord is one. Love the Lord your God with all your heart and with all your soul and with all your strength. These commandments that I give you today are to be on your hearts. Impress them on your children. Talk about them when you sit at home and when you walk along the road, when you lie down and when you get up. (Deut 6:4–7)

As Jesus walked, he normally talked. We see this on the road to Caesarea Philippi, in the grain fields, and on the road to Emmaus. He asked his disciples questions, he taught them about God, he astounded them with the depth of his simplicity.

But on this occasion was Jesus alone in his thoughts? Was he reliving scenes from his happy times with Lazarus? Did Jesus tell the disciples some of Lazarus's funniest stories, his corniest jokes, the best snippets of advice and counsel he had offered to Jesus? We are left to wonder about the heartbreak and grief bottled up inside of Jesus. Because he was fully man, Jesus was going through the stages of grief just like the rest of humanity.

Long before Kübler-Ross gave the world the language of grief, those aching like Jesus have traveled through the stages of denial, anger, bargaining, depression, and acceptance. Yet because Jesus was at the same time fully God, the way these feelings played out might have differed from the rest of the human race. Jesus knew death and bereavement were part of the human experience, part of the deal. A friendship that honors another in life should certainly do so in death as well. Jesus determined to honor God, and honor Lazarus, in the way he grieved. His manner of grief was a final tribute to the journey the two had made together. As the caravan made its way towards Jerusalem and then bent off to Bethany, Jesus modeled for his followers how to grieve for a friend.

The text next tells us that they finally arrived at Bethany and discovered Lazarus had been dead four days.[55] What a difficult homecoming for Jesus. For the first time, he was viewing the city of his best friend . . . without his friend. Upon arrival, Jesus avoided any fanfare. There was no triumphal entry into Bethany; Jesus stayed in the shadows on the outskirts of town. Remember, Bethany was only a stone's throw from Jerusalem and a price was placed upon his head there.

The text tells that "many Jews had come to Martha and Mary to comfort them in the loss of their brother."[56] The death of Lazarus was a "loss" to the sisters and to the community. "Loss" to an accountant leaves a negative balance—a deficit. "Loss" to an adjuster means a house has been destroyed. "Loss" to an athlete means their side had been defeated. "Loss" leaves everyone diminished and impacts the entire community, as John Donne reminds, "Any man's death diminishes me, / Because I am involved in mankind, /And therefore never send to know for whom the bell tolls; / It tolls for thee."[57] "Loss" was the only way anyone knew to keep score when death was the opponent—until Jesus' arrival at Bethany.

If Jesus went directly to the house crammed full with mourners, there could be no private conversation with his adopted family. Jesus paused instead at the bend in the road on the outskirts of town, sent a messenger in to scout out the sisters, and said, "Tell the sisters that I'm here." Martha received the message first. Don't you love Martha? One learns about Martha in Luke's Gospel; she was the logical sister, into every detail. She's the thinker, her sister Mary the feeler. Martha's the responsible one; she's task-oriented. She always has one more thing to do.

At that moment, Martha was probably the one arranging every detail. She had rearranged the flower sprays upon delivery, placed the obituary in the *Bethany Gazette* and *Jerusalem Post*, and prepared the remarks for the minister at a family prayer service. She was even secretly helping with the fried chicken and potato salad for the meal of the day for the mourners (but don't tell anyone). So when Martha heard the word that Jesus had *finally* arrived, she hurried to the outskirts of town to welcome him. Martha was a disciple of Jesus, so she did what disciples do when their Lord appears. She went out to meet him.[58]

Martha met Jesus, as her sister soon would, with an attitude towards him she had never felt before: supreme disappointment. In her eyes, Jesus had let the family down, betrayed the familial bond, and dishonored the relationship through his inaction. There was no conceivable excuse for it in her mind. It was a feeling for Jesus she had never before imagined she could have, and never before felt. But it was real, and it was all she could do not to despise him for it. How many times had they expressed love and affection for each other? How many meals shared? How many warm embraces? Jesus was there for every party, every holiday, and every major milestone worthy of celebration—but absent unaccountably when hardship struck. Was he a fair-weather friend all along, and the sisters too taken with him to notice? What category of friendship do they slot Jesus into now? Clearly, there had to be a better friend than the lowly Jesus. He was the friend, fairer than ten-thousand, who meant everything to them, but failed to appear at their greatest trial.

Eyeing Jesus for the first time since her telegram seemingly fell on deaf ears, certain words just exploded out of Martha's mouth. There was no way to contain this guttural outburst. "Jesus, if you had been here, my brother would not have died," she blurted. Was she angry? Yes, and she wanted him to know it. Disappointed? Obviously. Discouraged? Certainly. Forlorn? Yes. Wishing that Jesus had arrived earlier? No doubt.

Martha expressed cutting words to her friend Jesus: "If you had just been here, my brother would not have died!" In, with, and under them, one hears the cry of one once a king. Martha's words were the "cleaned up" version of David's cry of abandonment: "My God, My God, why have you forsaken me?"

She was too polite to say it quite that way. But it was what she was thinking—what she meant. And Jesus absorbed each body blow and every gut punch without response. Yet Martha then added, "But, Jesus, I know that God will do for you whatever you ask."

Why does she add that last phrase?

Her response confuses the reader a bit, and leaves much to conjecture. Perhaps she was wondering how she would now take care of her sister and herself. She had to be wondering, "Where is my future support going to come from? Who's going to provide for Mary and me? Lazarus was my brother, but also the breadwinner for our family. Lazarus was the one who provided for us." Social Security was not going to cut it. And so now she's saying, "I know, Jesus, that God will do for you whatever you ask." Lazarus is gone and you weren't here for him, but even now I know you can provide a way for us.

Martha's assessment was true: "If you had been here my brother would not have died, but even now God will grant you whatever you ask." No truer words had ever been spoken. There was no time in the ministry of Jesus where a person was dying and Jesus did not reverse the curse. There was never a time when Jesus threw up his hands, or claimed to be too tired for a healing that day. Thousands of years later, the words of Martha are no less true. If Jesus were physically present, death would have no hold on its victim. Death was no match for the Messiah, and Martha stated a fact she knew was more certain that death itself. If Jesus had been there, the end result would have been radically different. And even now, Martha was relying upon Jesus to take care of her and her sister. Yet, Jesus then spoke a reply appreciated only later, and never to be forgotten: "Your brother will rise again."

But hadn't she heard those same words Jesus just spoke, "Your brother will rise again," as a platitude already that day? Might a mourner not have said the same? In modern times the phrase of choice is, "I'm sorry for your loss." You hear it over and over throughout a modern-day visitation, and again after the internment. C. S. Lewis once exclaimed,

> Talk to me about the truth of religion and I'll listen gladly. Talk to me about the duty of religion and I'll listen submissively. But don't come talking to me about the consolations of religion or I shall suspect that you don't understand.[59]

There is a time when words meant to console simply do not provide consolation—the grief is too great. For Martha too, we can doubt it was the first time someone had tried to console her over these four long days with the words "Your brother will rise again." Every time the sisters went to synagogue, the faith community would recite the same eighteen prayers. And the second prayer spoken said, "You, O Lord, are mighty forever for you give life to the dead." It was the Pharisees who taught there would be a resurrection, and Martha knew the teaching well. She even believed it.

Martha was just walking in dance step with Jesus when she answered in the polite and proper way, "Yes, I know he will rise again at the resurrection on the last day." Martha believed resurrection would come one far and distant day. Hers was not yet a "sure and certain hope of the resurrection of the dead," but more a fuzzy, nebulous, and hazy optimism that somehow things will work out in the end. She had read and claimed the passage in Psalm 23 where David closes, "And I will dwell in the house of the Lord forever." She knew that resurrection and eternal life stood faithfully in the far distance. Martha reasoned aloud, "I know he'll rise again on the last day. I know when everyone else who has been faithful rises, then my brother will rise too."

Jesus then looked into her soul and spoke these all-powerful words:

> Martha, I am the resurrection and the life. He who believes in me
> will live, even though he dies; and whoever lives and believes in
> me will never die.

Let the audacity of the claim of those words sink in a moment:

I am the resurrection and the life.

In earlier days, it was the words "I AM" that touched off the firestorm placing Jesus on Jerusalem's "Most Wanted" list. He used "I am" in compound ways to speak of himself: "I am the bread of life," "I am the light of the world," "I am the door," "I am the good shepherd," and now, "I am the resurrection and the life"—with "I am the way, the truth and the life" and "I am the true vine" still to follow. But it was in John 8, that Jesus entered into a dialogue that placed a bazooka-sized target on his back. Jesus spoke saying:

> Your father Abraham rejoiced at the thought of seeing my day; he
> saw it and was glad." "You are not yet fifty years old," they said to
> him, "and you have seen Abraham!" "Very truly I tell you," Jesus
> answered, "before Abraham was born, I am!" At this, they picked
> up stones to stone him, but Jesus hid himself, slipping away from
> the temple grounds. (John 8:56–58)

Abraham, the Father of Israel and modern Judaism, was born around 1900 BC in ancient Ur—located in modern Iraq. He grew up worshiping the moon god Sin, but then became a follower of a God he called "the Lord, God Most High, Creator of Heaven and Earth."[60] About six hundred years after Abraham, the descendants of Abraham, now called "Hebrews," went down to Egypt because of a famine. There they were enslaved for four hundred years until Abraham's God raised up a leader named Moses to deliver the people. God spoke to Moses and commissioned him to lead the

Hebrews out of Egypt at a burning bush in the Egyptian Sinai. Speaking to God within the burning bush that was not consumed, Moses asked the God of Abraham his true name—his truest identity. God said to Moses, "I AM WHO I AM. This is what you are to say to the Israelites: 'I AM has sent me to you.'"[61] This description of God as I AM, "YHWH" in Hebrew (in English we get "Yahweh" and "Jehovah" from attempts to add vowels to this sacred name), at that moment became the most divine of names, so sacred it went unspoken by the Jewish people and was spelled without vowels (G-d) to make sure it was not read or recited even to this day. In a Jewish commentary called the Mishna, rabbis explained that the divine name means "I will be what the situation demands."

When Jesus later arrived on the scene, he not only spoke the sacred name, but he used it to speak of himself as synonymous with the Almighty God. Jesus claimed HE was God's final response to what every situation demanded. This was certainly blasphemy—unless it was true. Saint Anthanasius announced this truth in a "Homily on the Resurrection of Lazarus" when he proclaimed of Jesus,

> I am the voice of life that wakens the dead. I am the good odor that takes away the foul odor. I am the voice of joy that takes away the sorrow and grief. . . . I am the comfort of those who are in grief. Those who belong to me are given joy by me. I am the the joy of the whole world. I gladden all my friends and rejoice with them. I am the bread of life.[62]

To say "I am" and mean "I AM" meant Jesus was claiming deity. Jesus was claiming to be God in every moment, responding as God to whatever the situation demanded. And now, at this moment, the Lazarus situation demanded resurrection. A resurrection that meant far more than what most modern believers realize.

The word for "resurrection" in the Greek is *anastasis*: a standing up, a raising up from death to life again, a bodily rising. This word was never used to merely mean "life after death." Resurrection was used "to denote new bodily life *after* whatever sort of life after death there might be. . . . Referring to a two-step narrative in which resurrection, meaning new bodily life, would be proceeded by an interim period of bodily death. *Resurrection* wasn't, then, a dramatic or vivid way of talking about the state people went into immediately after death. It denoted something that might happen sometime *after* that."[63]

Apart from occasional mentions like 2 Maccabees 7, resurrection was a peripheral topic for the people of the intertestamental period (the four hundred years between the Old Testament and New Testament—the gap before Jesus arrived). By the time of Jesus and the early church, "resurrection language" had moved from the periphery to the center. In the time of Jesus, there were some Jews who agreed with pagan philosophers and denied any kind of future life—especially one that involved being reembodied. Socrates and Plato had presented the possibility of mortals becoming disembodied spirits detached from a bodily existence with an immortal soul. The Jewish group called the Sadducees were famous for denying a reembodiment after death—denying a bodily resurrection in the future.

But most Jews of Jesus' day believed in some type of eventual resurrection—"that is that God would look after the soul after death until, at the last day, God would give his people new bodies when he judged and remade the world. . . . That is what *resurrection* meant."[64] This is what Paul meant when he wrote, "And if the Spirit of him who raised Jesus from the dead is living in you, he who raised Christ from the dead will also give *life to your mortal bodies* through his Spirit, who lives in you."[65] N. T. Wright explains that when Jesus claimed to be the resurrection he was thus saying, "I am Life *after* life after death."[66]

He who believes in me will live, even though he dies.

But Jesus' claim to Martha is even more than this. Jesus is Resurrection and he is Life. The one who trusts in Jesus will live the life that is really living. Not only will Lazarus, through his believing faith, receive a reembodied presence in the days to come (after death and the eternal existence he is living beyond the grave), but the best life (*zoe* in the Greek) awaits him even now as well. Though Martha and Mary saw Lazarus as dead, just a corpse, the eternal truth of the matter was that he was closer to God, and more alive in God, than ever before. The grave had no claim upon Lazarus's life with God; the *zoe*-life continued beyond the grave and would do so even into the reembodied life to come. Lazarus, as a believer in Jesus, would never experience more of the best life (*zoe*) than he was experiencing at that moment. In Jesus, Lazarus was experiencing (even then) the life he had always dreamed of, the one for which he was created. Lazarus was living the good life, the best life, the one Jesus painted for his followers in the Beatitudes at the beginning of the Sermon on the Mount. Lazarus was experiencing life beyond the grave as *zoe,* the blessed life, his beatification. Being alive to God *is* really living.

And whoever lives and believes in me will never die.

The dream of never dying is a longing placed in each person by God before the garden of Eden. Most of humankind longs to live forever and to never die (in a body that doesn't wear out by the way!).[67] Recall that there were two trees in the center of the garden, one giving a knowledge of good and evil, the other the promise of life eternal. Through the ages, this quest for eternal life led some to try and trick the gods into granting it, and others to search uninhabited spaces for the famed Fountain of Youth. But Jesus announced that being eternally alive is a sure and certain promise for all who live trusting in him. There will be no time when the believer ceases to be "living on" and vibrantly alive in God. Death of the physical body in no way terminates the real person, nor does it break or harm the relationship between God and his people. "Precious in the sight of God is the death of his saints."[68] Later the apostle Paul explained Jesus' words this way: "I am convinced that neither death nor life, neither angels nor demons, neither the present nor the future, nor any powers, neither height nor depth, nor anything else in all of creation, will be able to separate us from the love of God that is in Jesus Christ our Lord."[69] Once a person is alive in Jesus, nothing separates that relationship.

Nothing.

NO MAN IS AN ISLAND

> No man is an island,
> Entire of itself,
> Every man is a piece of the continent,
> A part of the main.
> If a clod be washed away by the sea,
> Europe is the less,
> As well as if a promontory were.
> As well as if a manor of thy friend's
> Or of thine own were:
> Any man's death diminishes me,
> Because I am involved in mankind,
> And therefore never send to know for whom the bell tolls;
> It tolls for thee.
>
> —John Donne (1572-1631)[70]

Jesus said to her, "I am the resurrection and the life. The one who believes in me will live, even though they die; [26] and whoever lives by believing in me will never die. Do you believe this?"

[27] "Yes, Lord," she replied, "I believe that you are the Messiah, the Son of God, who is to come into the world."

[28] After she had said this, she went back and called her sister Mary aside. "The Teacher is here," she said, "and is asking for you." [29] When Mary heard this, she got up quickly and went to him. [30] Now Jesus had not yet entered the village, but was still at the place where Martha had met him. [31] When the Jews who had been with Mary in the house, comforting her, noticed how quickly she got up and went out, they followed her, supposing she was going to the tomb to mourn there.

[32] When Mary reached the place where Jesus was and saw him, she fell at his feet and said, "Lord, if you had been here, my brother would not have died."

—JOHN 11:25–32

CHAPTER SEVEN

Why Would God Allow It?

Where were you when I laid the earth's foundation? Tell me, if you understand. Who marked off its dimensions? Surely you know! Who stretched a measuring line across it?. . . Have you journeyed to the springs of the sea or walked in the recesses of the deep? Have the gates of death been shown to you? Have you seen the gates of the deepest darkness? Have you comprehended the vast expanses of the earth? Tell me, if you know all this.

—JOB 38:3–18

You never know how much you really believe anything until its truth or falsehood becomes a matter of life and death to you.

—C. S. LEWIS

As MARTHA STOOD LISTENING, Jesus spoke slowly, letting the words sink in for deep effect. "Martha, I am *the* resurrection and *the* life. If you die trusting in me, you live again. If you're living trusting in me, you'll never die." And then he asked this sister, his adopted sister, the question of all questions. "Do you believe it?" Emphasis upon "*you*."

Jesus was asking Martha if she would still trust him. Martha answered in simple trusting faith, "Yes Lord!" If Jesus was Lord then the answer to all the most difficult questions had to be "Yes." No need checking the back of the book for the answers, all the answers were "Yes!"[71] Martha then articulated the core that centered her life, even in the most challenging of moments,

> I have believed, and I still believe, because I know that you are the Messiah, the Son of God, the one God sent into the world.

Her words were the rock-solid foundation, on which the wise man built a house. They were the sure and certain hope by which Martha gained an eternal home. They became the profession of faith, an early creedal formula, for all who would follow Jesus into and through the waters of baptism and into new life. Examine them closely.

"Yes Lord!" is the answer of choice for disciples who most closely follow Jesus. It was the answer of the disciples when Jesus bid them fish from the other side of the boat. It was their answer when Jesus called them to follow. It was the answer of Peter when paying taxes with a coin found in a fish's mouth, and it was the widow from Zarephath's answer that resulted in the healing of her son. Only once did a follower of Jesus answer with, "No Lord." Unsurprisingly, it was Peter—and was the wrong answer even then. One day around noon Peter was on a rooftop when a sheet came down with kosher and un-kosher animals upon it. He heard a voice, "Kill and eat," and replied, "No Lord!" Peter placed dietary laws above Lordship and had to be corrected: "If Christ calls it clean then it is clean indeed." Whatever Jesus asks of his followers, the answer, as with Martha, must always be "Yes." This is why Paul instructs the Corinthians, "For no matter how many promises God has made, they are 'Yes' in Christ. And so through him the 'Amen' [meaning 'May it be so!'] is spoken by us to the glory of God."[72] Martha knew from past experience that the answers were always "Yes" in Jesus.

Martha's *"I believe"* was far more than merely mental assent to a fact. The word in the Greek comes from the root *pisteuo* and means "to have strong conviction, to commit or to put one's trust with."[73] The word is a favorite of John's—occurring fifteen times in his narrative—and is best understood as "ultimate trust or loyalty." For John, "believing" was the key. It could be easy for someone to say "I think," but not to say "I believe." Anyone can "think" the ice on the pond is thick enough to walk upon while standing safely on the bank. In John's Gospel, if someone "believes" ice is thick enough, they must place trust in it and venture out onto it in "ultimate trust."

In John's Gospel, *believe* is the key word used to describe a life totally entrusted to Jesus as Savior, Lord, and God. John's Gospel was written for no other purpose: "These things are written that you may believe that Jesus is the Christ, the Son of God, and that by believing you may have life in his name."[74]

Martha saw Jesus as the true "Messiah" who was to come into the world. This is nothing less than a Jewish geopolitical claim that Jesus was God's "anointed one," the promised coming king. In Israel, leaders were anointed with oil on the head and given a title. Priests were anointed, prophets were anointed, and kings were certainly anointed—and often then called "the anointed of God." Ever since Moses's day as leader of God's people, the Israelites had waited expectantly for another to come like Moses—to be the leader of leaders and the anointed of all anointed. This is what Martha meant by "the Messiah." Just before he died, Moses proclaimed God's promise, "I will raise up for them a prophet like Moses from among their brothers; I will put my words in his mouth and he will tell them everything I command him."[75] Prophecies about the coming messiah[76] were regularly discussed in synagogues and created both a longing and an expectation that God would soon come and rescue his people again—as he had done in the days of Moses. Martha, through her words, was affirming the anointing God had placed upon Jesus: "You are the Messiah, the Coming King."

But Martha said even more: You are not just the Jewish Messiah, but also the "Son of God" who was to come into the world. This was a Roman geopolitical statement of great significance. In Latin, there are two designations for a god: *deus* was the higher form for the classical gods and goddesses and *divus* was the lower form for lesser gods. Roman emperors used this lower form of Latin (*divus*) to speak of themselves as part of the god-system. However, in Greek there was not two words for "god," just the one word, *theos*. Living emperors first called the earlier dead emperors a Latin *divus* or god, but later used the term to speak of themselves even while living as *divus*. The living emperor was part of the god-system of the Romans. Romans were to worship their emperors. But in the days of Jesus, very few people spoke Latin, while everyone spoke Greek. So the emperor began to be called a *theos*, "a god." This was especially true of the emperor at the time of Jesus' birth, Augustus Caesar—who was referred to as "the Emperor Caesar, son of god, Augustus, ruler of all land and sea." Augustus later gave way to his son, Tiberius Caesar. He was the emperor during Jesus' ministry. One day in the temple, Jesus referred to a coin with Tiberius Caesar's inscription upon it when Israel's leaders were trying to entrap Jesus in his words.[77] Jesus asked for a denarius coin to be brought to him and queried, "Whose image and inscription is this?" The image on the coin would have

been Tiberius Caesar, and Jesus then said, "Give to Caesar what is Caesar's."
Most interesting is what the inscription on the coin would say in Greek. On
the front, the coin said "Tiberius Caesar, son of the divine Augustus." The
reverse side of the coin read "Greatest Priest" in Latin, but in Greek it read
"*theou huios*" ("god the son" or "son of god"). When Martha pronounced
Jesus to be the "Son of God" she was announcing *he* was the rightful ruler
of this world—*not* the emperor.

The church father Origen proposed years later that what occurred between Martha and Jesus was actually not a question at all, but a confirma-
tion of the faith seen in Martha by Jesus. "The Savior does not inquire, 'Do
you believe this?' in ignorance as to whether Martha did or did not believe
what was said. He did so in order that we, or indeed those who were then
present, might learn from her answer what her disposition was."[78] Origen
viewed Jesus' words not as a question, but as a statement: "You believe this."
Martha then completed the Savior's statement by adding, "Yes Lord, and
not only do I believe what you now say, but I believe now that you are the
Christ, something I also believed before. And I believe that you are the Son
of God who comes into the world and lives with all who believe in you."[79]

> Yes Lord! I believe that you are the Messiah, the Son of God, who
> was to come into the world.

With that, Martha turned around and went back into town, arriving
back home with a change in disposition. There she tried to whisper dis-
creetly to her sister, "Mary, the rabbi is here. Jesus is here asking for you."
But at the discreet news, Mary, the feeler, the dramatic one, jumped up
from her seat with artistic flair and made a straight path to Jesus. And when
Mary jumped up, like rabbits the community of mourners constantly filling
the home jumped up too to follow her.

In the days of Jesus, the comforting work of mourners was a pious act
and highly regarded as pleasing God. These spiritual mothers and fathers
knew a truth often forgotten in later days—grief and agony should not be
carried alone. These feelings of being "alone" can be overwhelming, and so
faithful friends and spiritual family show up in the waiting rooms of life. For
the three days prior to Jesus' arrival, the mourners were engaged in "days of
weeping" joining with tears in the agony of the bereaved. But on day four (the
day Jesus arrived) the mourners entered into four days of "heavy mourning"
but not with the tears of the first three days. "Light mourning" would then

continue from day eight through day thirty as the community checked in regularly on the one experiencing the disorientation of loss.[80]

Some faith communities have a name for members who care enough to carry the burdens of those in grief—"Bearer Groups." Taking their name from the four men who carried the paralytic to Jesus, these members of the Jesus community see themselves as ones who "bear the grief burdens of others," fulfilling the law of Christ. Because they knew only the presence of Jesus and the comfort of the Holy Spirit can bring healing to those in grief, "Bearer Groups" began to carry those who mourn to the One who *can* truly comfort them. There is a present (a gift of great value) in the often-silent presence of those who show up to be present as burden bearers—especially in times of great grief. Part of what makes social isolation and quarantine so difficult is not being able to bear the pain of others in their grief. The mourning community jumped up to follow Mary in her grief, reasoning, "Oh, she's so overcome with grief that she's headed to the tomb. We'd better go after her so we can comfort her there."

Picture the scene. Martha coming in, Mary popping up and running out the door, the mourners chasing after her, with Mary headed to the bend in the road because she wanted to talk to Jesus. And once arriving there, she couldn't help but express the exact words Martha had already revealed. All week long, over and over, sister had said to sister, "If Jesus had just been here." And when Mary finally had the opportunity, she thought she'd look squarely at Jesus and then say with all candor and honesty the words she had rehearsed, "Jesus, if you'd just been here this would not have happened." But when she actually saw her Lord, she did something else instead.

She fell at Jesus' feet.

On her knees, Mary modeled for all who come after her how best to question God when they know not what he's doing. Mary framed her confusion, and her doubt, in what she knew to be true. Jesus had not responded the way she hoped, and did not come when he was called. Jesus did not fit in the sisters' box nor come like a genie when his lamp was rubbed. But Mary still knew he was Teacher, he was Lord, and he was still good. So, she fell at Jesus' feet and uttered the words she felt so deeply all week: "Lord, if you had been here, my brother would not have died." She said the same words as her sister, but her posture was one of adoration.

Martha's a thinker. She's going to talk logically and rationally to Jesus. She's going to treat him with the respect of a Messiah. But she's going to ask the direct question, "Why weren't you here, and what's going on?"

Mary is a feeler, to whom worship might come more easily. Mary feels and knows exactly what Martha does and wants to express the same ideas as her sister. But seeing Jesus, her first response was to fall at the feet of Jesus in honor and worship. Even in the midst of her doubt, even in the midst of her despair, Mary framed her questions about Jesus' actions with truths she knew to be certain about his person and character. Instead of becoming an agnostic and doubting the entirety of the divinity of Jesus, Martha and Mary maintained faith in the midst of great questions. They rehearsed what they knew to be certain about Jesus—even when his actions perplexed and disappointed them. Pain eventually turned both sisters to God, and to ascribing to God the goodness due his name, even when there was much they did not understand.

If Martha and Mary could be honest and forthright what would they really say? Polite though they may be, Martha and Mary had to be at least a little put out (i.e., angry) with Jesus, and with God. If so, they would not be the first to get mad at God on occasion: Job did at the great loss he suffered, Jonah did over a hated enemy repenting and a worm eating his favorite bush (lame as that sounds), King David did over the death of priests carrying the ark and over the slaughter of people over a census question, and Hannah, Sarah, and Tamar probably did too over children not coming in the prime of their mothering years. At the wedding feast in Cana Jesus changed his mind and changed his plan at the request of his mother.81 All it took was a look, that look, from mom. Then came a message to the servants, "Do whatever he tells you," and water was soon flowing as wine. Why did Jesus come to the aid of some embarrassed newlyweds but not to the sisters in his adopted family?

When mom asked, things got done. When the sisters begged, nothing. All was quiet. Crickets.

How does one deal with the seeming unfairness of God? Teresa of Avila was once thrown from her carriage, slammed to the ground with a thud and then deposited into a mud puddle. At this she threw up her hands and questioned the providence of God. Teresa said God answered her, "This is how I treat all my friends." Teresa offered a quick and tart reply, "Then Lord it is not surprising you have so few friends."82 Even one raised to sainthood status doesn't sweetly smile when God launches them into mud puddles. Pigs do, but people question what a supposedly "good" God is up to. We wonder if our suffering is worth it—not knowing the rest of the story yet.

Where should followers stand when it comes to doubt and the difficult questions of life? Doubting God doesn't make him doubt anyone. Heartfelt questioning doesn't upset him. Why shouldn't others in doubt join the ranks of Martha and Mary? Believers facing life and death matters can almost universally say, "God, this is what I know to be true about you. This is what I know you've revealed to me. I have taken my stand right here. I know that you're the Messiah, I know that you're the holy one of God, but I don't understand what you're doing right now. And frankly I don't like it either."

If stated in that way, Jesus and his Father can absorb any doubts or questions just fine—even questions of isolation, quarantines, social distancing, and global pandemics. "My God, my God" is, after all, an affirmation of faith. "Why have you forsaken me?" acknowledges we are puzzled when God, in our view, makes no sense—and life spins out of control.

Honestly, a God too big to always make sense is exactly what is needed.

ALONE

> From childhood's hour I have not been
> As others were—I have not seen
> As others saw—I could not bring
> My passions from a common spring—
> From the same source I have not taken
> My sorrow—I could not awaken
> My heart to joy at the same tone—
> And all I lov'd—*I* lov'd alone—
> *Then*—in my childhood—in the dawn
> Of a most stormy life—was drawn
> From ev'ry depth of good and ill
> The mystery which binds me still—
> From the torrent, or the fountain—
> From the red cliff of the mountain—
> From the sun that 'round me roll'd
> In its autumn tint of gold—
> From the lightning in the sky
> As it pass'd me flying by—
> From the thunder, and the storm—
> And the cloud that took the form
> (When the rest of Heaven was blue)
> Of a demon in my view—
>
> —Edgar Allan Poe (1809–1849)[83]

When Mary reached the place where Jesus was and saw him, she fell at his feet and said, "Lord, if you had been here, my brother would not have died." 33 When Jesus saw her weeping, and the Jews who had come along with her also weeping, he was deeply moved in spirit and troubled. 34 "Where have you laid him?" he asked.

"Come and see, Lord," they replied. 35 Jesus wept.

36 Then the Jews said, "See how he loved him!" 37 But some of them said, "Could not he who opened the eyes of the blind man have kept this man from dying?"

38 Jesus, once more deeply moved, came to the tomb. It was a cave with a stone laid across the entrance. 39 "Take away the stone," he said. "But, Lord," said Martha, the sister of the dead man, "by this time there is a bad odor, for he has been there four days." 40 Then Jesus said, "Did I not tell you that if you believe, you will see the glory of God?"

41 So they took away the stone. Then Jesus looked up and said, "Father, I thank you that you have heard me. 42 I knew that you always hear me, but I said this for the benefit of the people standing here, that they may believe that you sent me."

—JOHN 11:32–42

CHAPTER EIGHT

The Tears of God

Sing the praises of the Lord, you his faithful people; praise his holy name. For his anger lasts only a moment, but his favor lasts a lifetime; weeping may stay for the night, but rejoicing comes in the morning.

—Ps 30:4–5

Those who sow in tears will reap with songs of joy. He who goes out weeping, carrying seed to sow, will return with songs of joy, carrying sheaves with him.

—Ps 126:5–6

MARY FELL AT JESUS' feet and said the honest-to-God words that had bothered her for days: "Lord, if you had been here, my brother would not have died." Jesus looked down at his feet and saw her weeping there (a place she would be again a few weeks later), then he looked up to see the mourners who had followed her heavy with tears as well. This was the way of the weeping, a caravan of consolation, the people of God realizing the truth of Solomon's words, "There is a time for everything, and a season for every activity under heaven: a time to be born, and a time to die . . . a time to weep and a time to laugh, a time to mourn and a time to dance," and this was the time to mourn. Solomon goes on to say, "I have seen the burden God has laid upon mankind. He has made everything beautiful in its time. He has also set eternity in the hearts of men, yet they cannot fathom what God has done from beginning to end."[84] There is a beautiful time for every activity, including a time to weep. God makes it beautiful, despite the fact that we cannot fathom exactly what God is doing.

At this moment, Jesus experienced the strongest feeling of raw emotion found anywhere in the Gospels. "When Jesus saw Mary weeping, and the Jews who had come along with her also weeping, he was deeply moved in spirit and troubled."[85] Jesus felt, in all who surrounded him with tears, the grief of those who mourn *without* hope. Jesus absorbed the hopelessness. Later the apostle Paul would write, "Brothers and sisters, we do not want you to be ignorant about those who fall asleep, or to grieve like the rest of mankind, who have no hope."[86] Soon Christ-followers would have a reason to mourn differently, to mourn with hope; but what Jesus absorbed within himself that day was the hopelessness and despair of utter loss. They wept as if they had lost, as if the game was over and the home team had come up short again. To the folks of Bethany, the virus that had invaded Lazarus's body had won—Lazarus, and all who loved him, had lost.

Experiencing this, Jesus' heart ached with anguish and he was angry, "deeply moved in spirit and troubled." The word used for "deeply moved" in the Greek is the same one used for the snorting of an upset horse; it generally means "to snort with anger or to have indignation." Here it describes a Savior who hates what death has done to the human race. Jesus snorts back at death and the devil behind this deed, and he is "troubled." That word in the Greek, *tarasso*, describes "an inward commotion, a disturbance"—a nauseous feeling. Seeing first-hand, up close and personally what a virus of death rot upon the human race stoked the righteous indignation inside of Jesus—while he also absorbed a sucker punch to the gut.

Feeling angry and nauseous, Jesus asked, "Where have you laid him?"

"Come and see, Lord," they said. And this reply must have caught Jesus off guard as well. Those were *his* words, to his earliest disciples—the first Jesus uttered in the Gospel of John. Isn't it interesting that John's Gospel begins with the earliest disciples tagging along behind Jesus at the encouragement of John the Baptist? Jesus turned to the followers and asked, "What do you want?" The disciples then inquired, "Where do you abide? Where is your home?" And Jesus reply was simply, "Come and you will see."[87] Jesus invited these earliest followers to spend the day with him and experience the God-life, the life that is truly living. It was the life for which they were created. Now, three years later, it is Jesus who comes into town and asks the question, "Where is Lazarus abiding?" The same response Jesus had once given now greets him: "Come and you will see." Jesus invited his first followers to join him in a journey toward abundant life. In Bethany, the townspeople invited Jesus to follow them into an encounter with death. Little did they realize the "life of the funeral" had come upon the scene. The phrase "better late than never" hardly begins to capture how better this late arrival could make things.

Jesus followed them to the tomb and absorbed all the raw emotion on display. Then, "Jesus wept."

Jesus was overcome with indescribable grief and it all spilled out. His tears were not the loud, wailing type of Mary and the mourners, but a quiet shedding of tears. This was no show, no public relations ploy to get back in good with the sisters. They were quiet tears that served as a billboard to a grieving world. In Greek culture, and in Eastern religions, there is one certainty about deity: a god, without doubt, will not feel pain or pathos for the human race. A god does not hurt. And a god certainly does not take upon himself (absorb) the pain of others. If a human goes through a difficult time feeling *pathos*, a god will be *a-pathos* (apathetic) about entering into the pain in any way. The pantheon of Greek gods is completely apathetic—they do not care. Into that standard, John introduced a story that differs: "Oh, really is that what your gods do? Let me introduce you to the true God. Look at Jesus, absorbing within the pain of others, and taking their grief and pain upon himself. Look, and see in him the tears of God."

The tears streamed down. Most people approved, saying, "Look how much he loved his friend Lazarus." Men often refuse to cry in public, but not Jesus. Public tears elicit a plethora of responses from those who see them: grief, love, disdain, pity, and, most painful of all to the one crying, embarrassment. One day King David, dressed only in a linen ephod (holy boxers?) "danced before the Lord with all his might while he and the entire house of Israel brought up the ark of the Lord with shouts and the sound of trumpets."[88] David put himself out there to honor God and let his real emotions pour out. He was a man with a heart like God's. But David's wife Michal watched David's dance from a palace window. And when she saw King David "leaping and dancing before the Lord, she despised him in her heart."[89] Michal was embarrassed by King David's actions, but God and the people loved him for it.

Tears are like that; the problem is generally not with the tearful one, but in the heart of the one embarrassed by them. Jesus wept for the first time here, and then a few weeks later weeps again over Jerusalem as he enters the Holy City for the last time.[90] Then days later he'll weep again in the garden of Gethsemane as he agonizes over the cup of sin he will be called upon to drink. Real men do cry, especially the one fully God and fully man.

But others began to taunt his tears instead: "If he loved him so much, why didn't he do something about it while Lazarus was still alive? He took care of the blind man, but he didn't take care of Lazarus when he got the virus?" This is the first time in the account that the great apologetic dilemma surrounding God and Jesus is introduced. It is based upon three statements, all of which are true: a) God is good and acts in good ways, b) God is all-powerful and there is nothing he cannot do, and c) Mankind experiences pain and suffering and people die. Why?

The great question of the ages, "Why does a good God allow his children to suffer?" was being asked again now—of Jesus. Lazarus was the case study, Bethany the petri dish. A few solve this moral dilemma by claiming that God is not *all* good—like the Greek gods, his "goodness" is relative and subject to his own interest. Others like Elie Wiesel speak about a good God in the past tense and suppose the God that was all good has died and is no more (this is his explanation for atrocities like the Holocaust). Quite a few religious folks (including a rabbi named Harold Kushner) propose that God is indeed all good, but is not all powerful . . . yet. Kushner proposes a type of "randomness" that exists in the world that is beyond the power and control of God at this time, but someday will be subdued by God in the last days. In the case of a global pandemic, this argument would be that God wants to do something about it but cannot yet control the contagion. In the short-term, Kushner sees a God not yet able to provide a cure. This version of God has him "good," and deeply caring—but not yet all-powerful. John chooses none of these answers . . . that do not answer. Instead, John presents this moral dilemma as the question of all questions—the one at the epicenter of life and death. But John doesn't care to directly answer it. The entire episode serves as John's answer to the great dilemma, whether a coronavirus, a cancer, or a calamitous or capricious act be the driver of the moral dilemma.

Jesus arrived at the tomb and was once again overcome with the same troubled emotion as before. Seeing the tomb of his beloved friend, after missing the funeral due to his God-imposed quarantine, must have made the whole experience even more disturbing for him. By this time in life, Jesus had likely buried his father, taken over running the carpenter's shop for a season, and then passed it on to his brothers.[91] He knew what it was like to bury a parent older than he, but now he absorbs the gravity of having a friend (that you always thought would outlive you) die before you do. Looking at the tomb, this spot of ground held added significance for him simply because Lazarus, his friend, was laid to rest there. Ever since the great patriarch Abraham purchased the Cave of Machpelah to bury his beloved Sarah, the place of burial had great importance to Israel. A burial site conveyed a certain family heritage, a connectivity to the past, and served as an important reminder in the present that death was the destiny of everyone.

The tomb of Lazarus's family was a cave with a stone rolled across the entrance (any visitor to Bethany today can still enter inside.)[92] This tomb was a typical burial space for a Middle Eastern family—a cave carved out of a rock ledge. The cave would serve an entire family for generations to come, not just a single individual as was common later. Lazarus's parents and grandparents were most likely buried inside the family tomb well before him. Remember that Jews do not embalm, and so the effects of death begin immediately as the body begins to quickly decompose in the hot, arid conditions. That is why Lazarus's funeral occurred immediately after his death and while Jesus was still far away in self-isolation.

The cave was divided into separate areas for different stages of the burial process. Because of this, the tomb contained a set of stairs that led through the doorway from outside and into the tomb itself. There one entered into the *weeping chamber*, where family and friends could weep on the first three days after death. This was an extremely significant time, because in Jesus' day there was a Jewish belief that when anyone died, the soul of the dead person lingered in the vicinity of the body for three days. But by the fourth day, the soul had certainly departed, and there was then no possibility that the soul might reenter the body and resuscitation take place. Four days after death meant that the person was completely dead and would stay dead—all hope was officially lost.

Across from the weeping chamber, the body of the deceased would be in a connecting room called the *burial chamber*. There, the corpse would be placed on one of the burial niches carved into the cave wall. Lazarus would be placed in a niche, wrapped in strips of linen treated with perfume and with a head covering over his face. Spices would then be piled upon the corpse in order to hide the stench as the body began to slowly decay. After three days, the stone across the tomb would be secured in place and no one would enter again for a year or so. On the one-year anniversary of the death, after the body had fully decayed, the family would reenter the tomb and place the remaining bones in an ossuary (a small stone "bone box" with the person's name on it). The ossuary would then be placed in a spot in the back of the tomb, often called an *antechamber*—entered through a small door where the boxes would be stacked like boxes in a modern attic. There would be a personalized stone ossuary for every family member buried within the tomb.[93]

Moved again with deep emotion, Jesus commanded the townspeople, "Remove the stone. Roll it away." Immediately Martha took issue with Jesus' directive, assuming he wanted to enter the weeping chamber and have a final moment with Lazarus. She understood Jesus might want a last glimpse of his friend, but she feared it would not go well (plus she was a high-control person). So Martha reminded Jesus, "By this time there is a bad odor, for he has been there four days." Lazarus was good and dead, all hope was lost, and decomposition was slowly altering his remains. With these words, Martha demonstrated the limited faith and confidence she had in Jesus in the short term. She was not expecting an imminent change of circumstances. Martha believed Jesus took care of people when living, but in her mind, Jesus could not do anything for people now so fully dead. If Jesus had showed up while Lazarus was alive, he could have cast out the virus and healed his sickness. If Jesus had even arrived immediately after death, he could have resuscitated Lazarus. But, in Martha's estimation, there was nothing Jesus could do now but take in the fumes of death and decay. "It's going to stink in there to high heaven," she might have said. "He's been in there for four days. Jesus, why would you want to go in there?"

Jesus turned and replied to Martha in prophetic tones, "You sent me a message. I sent you a response. Do you remember it? I said this will not end in death but that the glory of God will be revealed. That's what I told you was going to happen." And with that Martha stepped back. The stone across the tomb was rolled away, opening the underworld and releasing the stench contained within. Everyone expected Jesus to stoop and enter the tomb, but Jesus had no intention of stooping down, but instead looked up. "Looking up" was the natural posture that was prelude to Jesus' prayers. Earlier in John, Jesus "looked up" before multiplying the loaves and fishes. Later he will "look up" before offering his high priestly prayer.[94] Things in Bethany were looking up because Jesus was looking up—and praying a prayer through his tears.

Richard Foster explains, "Tears are God's way of helping us descend with the mind into the heart"; they are a gift that draws us closer to God.[95] Jesus was looking up and offering to God what his tears brought up from his heart into his head. A trio of Greek words, *klaio*, *pentheo*, and *dakruo*, describe the tears and godly sorrow of those who travel through this "prayer of tears" with Jesus. These words detail an experience most people strive to avoid. Yet tears are the frequent partner of the faithful now filling the pages of Scripture. Such stories continue on in the great saints who have longed for tears as well. This trio of Greek words speaks of weeping, tears, and sorrow that accompany a broken and contrite heart. There is grace in tears.

The men and women who grace the pages of the Bible were well acquainted with such gifts and graces. Job sets the tone when he declares, "My eyes pour out tears to God."[96] Isaiah is overcome with sorrow over the desolation of Israel and cries out, "I weep with the weeping of Jazer; I drench you with my tears."[97] Jeremiah prayed through the tears so often he was given the designation "the weeping prophet"—a reputation well deserved. Jeremiah carried the burden of God's people and moaned, "O that my head were a spring of water, and my eyes a fountain of tears, so that I might weep day and night for the slain of my poor people." Jeremiah was so full of weeping, tears and godly sorrow that he comprised an entire book of the Bible called Lamentations—it was filled with the prayer of tears. He proclaims there, "Let tears stream down like a torrent day and night! Give yourself no rest, your eyes no respite."[98]

And if Lamentations were not enough, one can hardly read a page that is not wet with tears in the Psalms. David writes, "I am weary with my moaning, every night I flood my bed with tears; I drench my couch with weeping." Pay attention and you will notice David is so convinced that his prayers of tears are effectual that he appeals to the tears he has shed as a witness to God: "You have kept count of my tossings; put my tears in your bottle. Are they not in your record?" He goes on to state, "My tears have been my food day and night" and confesses he even sheds tears over the disobedience of Israel: "My eyes shed streams of tears because your law is not kept."[99]

Jesus, who announced, "Blessed are those who mourn," and later, "Blessed are you who weep now,"[100] modeled this prayer of tears in his ministry. All this praying with tears could seem a bit depressing, especially if good feelings and an easy life are what one wants from the gospel. However, the saints of Scripture, and throughout Christian history, longed for tears—they sought them. They believed tears were a gift from God, a "charism of tears" to help better pray and beseech God with all one's being. For them, "the people most to be pitied were those who go through life with dry eyes and cold hearts"[101]—as the Prayer of Tears provides "deep joy" to an inner soul longing and thirsting for God.

Perhaps a window to this gift of tears is found in Jesus himself, who "offered up prayers and supplications, with loud cries and tears"[102] in the garden of Gethsemane a few weeks to come. We learn from Paul that Jesus' loud cries and tears were joined by the groaning and sighs of the Holy Spirit: "In the same way, the Spirit helps us in our weakness. We do not know what we ought to pray for, but the Spirit himself intercedes for us through wordless groans. And he who searches our hearts knows the mind of the Spirit, because the Spirit intercedes for God's people in accordance with the will of God."[103] For many saints, tears often indicated the intensity of the moment, its urgency. And as the saints pray through tears, the Holy Spirit interprets those tears in sighs and groans to God, conveying on our behalf the depth and full range of emotion embodied within our words. When words are not enough, the disciple's tears join with the Spirit's sighs in bringing a condition to the Father. In praying through tears, Jesus joined a long list of the faithful who knew this way of prayer.[104]

Through the tears, Jesus looked up and prayed, "I praise you, God, that you hear my prayer. And you always hear my prayers. I am praying this prayer so that everyone will know that you are listening to me." And when he finished the prayer, he did not go into the tomb. He didn't go inside to view a dead corpse. Instead he summoned from deep within a loud voice, and then shouted . . .

. . . and the world changed.

KATRINA'S SUNDIAL

Time is
Too Slow for those who Wait,
Too Swift for those who Fear,
Too Long for those who Grieve,
Too Short for those who Rejoice;
But for those who Love,
Time is not.

—Henry Van Dyke (1852–1933)[105]

When he had said this, Jesus called in a loud voice, "Lazarus, come out!" [44]
The dead man came out, his hands and feet wrapped with strips of linen, and a cloth around his face.

Jesus said to them, "Take off the grave clothes and let him go."

—JOHN 11:43–44

CHAPTER NINE

"The Rest of the Story"

The voice of the Lord is over the waters; the God of glory thunders, the Lord thunders over the mighty waters. The voice of the Lord is powerful; the voice of the Lord is majestic. The voice of the Lord breaks the cedars; the Lord breaks in pieces the cedars of Lebanon.... The voice of the Lord shakes the desert; the Lord shakes the Desert of Kadesh. The voice of the Lord twists the oaks and strips the forests bare. And in his temple all cry, "Glory!"

—Ps 29:3–9

MARTHA STEPPED BACK FROM protesting, and the stone was rolled away from the tomb. Saint Athanasius later described the scene this way:

> They took then the stone from the mouth of the tomb. The whole crowd marveled, witnessing the smell of pus of Lazarus, who was decayed. He had rotted so that they were not able to approach within the tomb because of the smell of its body and its decay. But into the midst came Jesus, the storehouse that is full of life, the mouth that is full of sweet odor, the tongue that frightens death, the Mighty One in his commands, the joy of those who are sorrowful, the rising of those who have fallen, the resurrection of the dead, the assembly of the strong, the hope of the hopeless.[106]

Jesus prayed aloud to his Father with "the tongue that frightens death" a prayer of thanksgiving for a deed not yet done—but with a conviction and certainty it had already been accomplished. When he finished praying,

Jesus thundered his command in a majestic voice loud enough to rattle the gates of Hades and wake the dead:

"Lazarus, come out!"

There was a pause.

Then a noise rose up from inside the cave as though something were stirring. Then came the sound of a man wrapped in linen cloths lumbering toward the door. The people heard the sounds, and an audible gasp filled the graveyard. They waited outside with baited breath until what no eye had ever seen, what no ear had ever heard, what no mind had ever conceived actually appeared. A man four days dead was now alive and walking out of death's tomb back into the land of the living. This was resurrection: life *after* life after death. The entire community stood spellbound as a body dead four days began wobbling towards them much like a zombie. Jesus then told the people standing there with their jaws hanging down, "Take his grave clothes off. Let him go."

Jesus *prayed*, and God listened. Toward the end of Psalm 22, well after David had penned "My God, my God, why have you forsaken me," one reads these words from him: "I will declare your name to my brothers, in the assembly I will praise you. You who fear the Lord, praise him! . . . For he has not despised or disdained the suffering of the afflicted one; he has not hidden his face from him, but has listened to his cry for help."[107] Jesus prayed, and God listened to his cry for help.

Jesus *shouted*, and an army of angels stood ready. David reminds all, "The voice of the Lord is powerful and majestic!" One of the early church fathers, Gregory of Nyssa, explained, "Here we have a man past the prime of life, a corpse, decaying, swollen, in fact already in a state of dissolution, so that even his own relatives did not want the Lord to draw near the tomb because the decayed body enclosed there was so offensive. And yet, he is brought into life by a single call."[108] Lazarus was now experiencing life after life after death. This is the same voice, the Logos, who spoke Creation into being:

> O power of the voice, arousing the four days dead as from sleep and bringing forth from the grave as well loosed and swiftly running the one who was bound with grave bands. Give your attention, beloved, to the voice, and you will find him to be the Word that spoke at the creation.[109]

This word for "shout" occurs only eight times in the entire Greek Bible—six times in John's Gospel. This is the first. Here, Jesus shouted through the open tomb into the unseen world to summon back his friend from the afterlife. Jesus shouted, and death became life anew. Soon, the crowds will gather in Jerusalem around Antonio's Fortress as Pilate will sit in judgment upon Jesus. On four different occasions this word for "shout" will be used there to speak of an angry mob longing to remove Jesus by sending him to the cross. Yet the Lazarus story foreshadows a day when Jesus will shout again:

> The Lord himself will descend with a shout, and with the voice of the archangel, and by a trumpet sound raise up the dead to incorruption—so now too he who is in the tomb, at the voice of the command, shakes off death as if it were only sleep. Jesus shouts; death becomes abundant life. The crowds will soon shout; and abundant life will be put to death.[110]

Lazarus, came out! "Lazarus, this is your wake-up call," Jesus announced. Where was Lazarus when Jesus called him, and in what kind of state? Evidently, Lazarus was in the "waiting room" of the dead, the place best understood in biblical terms as *Hades* (*Sheol* in Hebrew). This idea of Hades differs from the biblical "hell" as Hades is a "waiting place or abode of the dead," while hell is the eternal consequence of condemnation from God at the Last Judgment. Hades, then, is the state in which all the dead exist as they await final judgment on the Last Day. In the New Testament, a descent to Hades may simply refer to someone's death and disembodiment from an earthly body to a spiritual one. Here in John's story of Lazarus, Jesus does not descend into Hades, but by his voice summons Lazarus from Hades to return to his previous body as a living new creation. Jesus *will* later descend into Hades,[111] but this will occur after his death and during the three days as he awaits and/or announces his coming resurrection to the saints long waiting there.

Earlier in his ministry, Jesus told a parable of a rich man and a poor man—the poor man is curiously named "Lazarus."[112] In the parable (an artfully created story told for a spiritual purpose) Jesus tells of an unbridgeable chasm that separates the wicked and the righteous after death while all are in a place called Hades—with this Hades evidently divided into two halves. At death, the poor man Lazarus is placed next to the great Father Abraham, while the rich man is placed "far away" on the side of punishment where he longs for a drop of water to cool his tongue from the fire. In anguish, the rich man realized his woeful fate and what will soon befall his family. In his distress he cried out for Father Abraham to send his family members a sign that they may not receive his same punishment at death, but to no avail. In Jesus' parable, Hades is the place where the wicked dead reside and are already being punished. This punishment is in the intermediate state, for the bodily resurrection and the final judgment are still waiting in the future.[113]

Notice that comfort or punishment in the parable is applied to people in Hades, as they await the final resurrection. The Bible uses various terms to speak of the "waiting room" of the dead saints, awaiting a new bodily resurrection. The two most popular are "heaven" and "paradise." The parabolic Lazarus was in "heaven," in a "paradise garden," awaiting the final resurrection and judgment when the story occurs. Similarly, Jesus' true friend Lazarus was in the same exact place when Jesus bid him leave paradise and return again to this life. Also, notice in this parable that the dead in the waiting place are not disembodied spirits, but embodied spirits taking some type of bodily form.

To be clear, Lazarus was dead. He was asleep in the "waiting room" of Hades in his pre-resurrection body awaiting the Second Coming of the Lord. The only thing that could change his circumstances was a private wake-up call from Jesus. C. S. Lewis supposes Lazarus's new body to be the very opposite of a floating, disembodied spirit; he imagines a body "more solid, more real, more substantial than our present ones."[114] The embodied spirit of Lazarus in Hades was a new body, a new body in the process of complete transformation (the Greek word is *metamorphoō*) into the resurrected body Lazarus would hold for eternity. Paul will later explain, "And we, who with unveiled faces all reflect the Lord's glory, are being transformed [*metamorphoō*] into his likeness with ever-increasing glory, which comes from the Lord, who is the Spirit."[115] Like a moth that has entered into the cocoon, Lazarus was in the process of becoming God's "new creation." Lazarus was in the process of exchanging his physical body for a new, more glorious, spiritual body. This new body awaiting Lazarus was the one God intended for him from the beginning—free from sickness and not subject to any virus, death, or decay. Yet before that could be fulfilled, Jesus bid Lazarus return to his old body again.

Later in Scripture, Paul explains that the body we currently have is like an "earthly tent." While living in the "earthly tent," believers groan and are burdened because they long for an "eternal house, made by God," but do not want to step outside the earthly tent, into the cold of death, to enter the new dwelling.[116] It is the Spirit of God that reminds disciples that exchanging the "earthly tent" for the "heavenly dwelling" will be glorious. Lazarus, the best friend of Jesus, was asked to leave the "heavenly dwelling" and return again to the "earthly tent"—and was happy to do so. But why? Why would anyone willingly leave paradise to return to earth again? Simply put, because Lazarus's best friend and Savior was the one calling him back again.

Lazarus, come out! All the signs at the cemetery pointed "One Way," people died to enter but no one ever left. Jesus changed all that. In bidding Lazarus to "come out," Jesus was inviting his friend back to his side—the place where Lazarus most belonged. Lazarus was experiencing life *after* life after death, in order to be with Jesus. To "come out" for Lazarus was really to "come home"—to return to the place where life was most certain and secure. In awakening and coming out to meet Jesus, Lazarus turned what was only a cemetery into what would then forever be viewed as a "dormitory."[117]

Lazarus tomb was the dorm in which to sleep until Jesus called him back to his side again. Lazarus was asleep, but Jesus woke him. In so doing he transformed a place of death into a place for a sleepover. The church father Andrew of Crete may capture this concept best of all:

> Lazarus, Come out! It is the voice of the Lord, the proclamation of the King—an authoritative command. . . . Lazarus, Come out! Let them know that the time has come when those in the tombs will hear the voice of the Son of man. Once they have heard they will come alive. Come out! The stumbling block is taken away. Come to me—I am calling you. Come out! As a friend, I am calling you; as Lord I am commanding you. . . . Come out! Covered with the burial cloth so that they won't think you were only pretending to be dead. Let them see your hands and feet bound and your face covered. Let them see if they still do not believe the miracle. Come out! Let the stench of your body prove the resurrection. Let the burial linen be undone so that they can recognize the one who was put in the tomb. Come out! Come alive and enliven! Come out of the tomb. Teach them how all creation will be enlivened in a moment when the trumpet's voice proclaims the resurrection of the dead. Come out! Let breath appear in your nostrils, let blood pulse through your veins, let the voice sound in your larynx, let words fill your ears, let vision enlighten your eyes, let the sense of smell fill your senses, walk as nature intended as your earthly tent is enlivened by your soul. Come out! Leave behind the burial cloth and glorify the miracle. Leave the revolting stench of death

and proclaim the strength of my power. I'm calling you out! Come out.[118]

No more strange (or amazing) five simple words have ever been written: *"The dead man came out . . ."* It sounds so simple—yet so odd. The one once dead just walked out of the tomb. A dead man walking again. But he was not walking easily. He still wore the clothes of the dead and made his way back into the light with feet wrapped, body wound, and face covered. He needed to wriggle free of the confines of death, like a butterfly would the confines of a cocoon. To do so, he needed help to get free. So, Jesus said to the crowd, *"Take off the grave clothes and let him go."* Jesus was not playing a funny joke on Lazarus, nor encouraging the crowd to quickly unwind Lazarus into the first Christian streaker! Before they could take all the grave clothes off, someone had to run back to the house and find new clothes to put back on him. You can't "take off" without "putting on" as well.

The cloth around his face came off first—thus the one who was blind could now see life more clearly than ever before. His hands came free next, and the one who had lost touch with the living felt at home again. The feet were unwrapped, and the one once hobbled was now free to run and jump. And once they did fetch the new clothes, Lazarus slid a fresh robe over his head and down over his torso until they could unwind the linen from his most private areas—showing them honor. After that, the burial clothes went straight to be burned in the city dump as Lazarus's friends looked on in celebration.

THREE RESPONSES

The raising of Lazarus completed the Seven Signs in John's Gospel. This episode marked the transition from Jesus' ministry to his glorious death and resurrection—the central event to which each of the signs pointed. The response to the Lazarus event produced three distinct responses in the lives of those who witnessed it: *Belief, Bounty,* and *Beauty.* Each deserves to be considered in its own right.

Belief

Many put their ultimate trust in Jesus as their Messiah. As a result of the miraculous healing, "many of the Jews, who had come to visit Mary, and had seen what Jesus did, put their faith in him."[119] Remember from earlier that "Bethany was less than two miles from Jerusalem, and many Jews had come to Martha and Mary to comfort them."[120] These devoted Jews from Jerusalem were among the most devout religious people of any kind in the world. Most Jews of this day went to a synagogue daily to pray, read from the Torah, and discuss the teachings of the elders of the city. But these Jews could and would generally do more; they lived within eyesight of the temple and had access not just to a synagogue, but to the temple itself. In temple or in synagogue these locals could pray, listen to all the word of God be read, give alms, and join in the most thoughtful of discussions among leading rabbis, scribes, and priests. Each day, without fail, they would recite a set of prayers called in Hebrew the *Shimoneh Esrei*, or "Eighteen Benedictions." Among these daily prayers, Benediction Two stated, "You, O Lord, are mighty forever for you give life to the dead."[121] Benediction Fourteen concerned the Redemption of Jerusalem:

> To Jerusalem Thy city return Thou in mercy and dwell in her midst as Thou hast spoken, and build her speedily in our days as an everlasting structure and soon establish there the throne of David. Blessed be Thou, O Lord, the builder of Jerusalem.[122]

It was followed by Benediction Fifteen regarding the coming Messiah:

> The sprout of David Thy servant speedily cause Thou to sprout up; and his horn do Thou uplift through Thy victorious salvation; for Thy salvation we are hoping every day. Blessed be Thou, O Lord, who causest the horn of salvation to sprout forth.[123]

These prayers were a part of daily life as the Jews of Jesus' day awaited a new king, a messiah, or "anointed one." This messiah would return to redeem Jerusalem and restore the city as the Holy City of God and the nation as God's covenant people.

Many of the Jews gathered at the home of Mary and Martha would have earlier that morning gone to the temple or synagogue and recited those same benedictions. They rocked their entire bodies in a rhythmic cadence as they yearned in prayer for God to send a messiah to deliver the people and restore the city. After their prayers were finished, they traveled to Bethany to comfort and support the sisters in their season of grief. Soon, the young rabbi from Nazareth arrived on the outskirts of town and called for the sisters. Everyone followed Mary out for her meeting with Jesus, and then they all became witnesses to a resurrection. Many who saw it realized the prayers they had prayed so many times, and even again that morning, had come true. God had heard their cries, and Jesus was the long-awaited Messiah revealed! Realizing this, they placed their faith, and put their trust, in Jesus as the Holy One of God.

Bounty

Others decided Jesus was a nuisance and must be exterminated. The sun's same heat that melts butter also hardens clay. The Lazarus event brought a similar heat to the hearts of mankind. Some hearts were melted, and they quickly put their faith in Jesus as Messiah. But for others, the same event evoked a far different response: the hard-heartedness of self-preservation. John explained, "But some of them went to the Pharisees and told them what Jesus had done. Then the chief priests and the Pharisees called a meeting of the Sanhedrin."[124] Instead of Lazarus's healing eliciting praise to God and support for Jesus, the miracle had the opposite effect. It caused the Pharisees to fear a loss of influence inside a religious system beholden to the Roman Empire (not the Jewish messiah) for its status and affluence.

Interestingly, it was the Pharisees who were the great advocates of "resurrection"—it was one of the main planks in their party platform. They talked about resurrection, wrote about resurrection, and even argued about resurrection—a resurrection "out there" in the far distant future. But Jesus wasn't talking about "far off" resurrection; his version was happening now. Some people talk, but a few people, like Jesus, *do*. Jesus was authentic, and people were either drawn to authenticity or repelled by it. For most Pharisees, discovering someone more authentic than themselves is a heart-hardener. So, the Pharisees, instead of welcoming resurrection wherever God provided it, went looking for other religious leaders to help stomp it out.

The group of religious leaders, the Sanhedrin, gathered at the temple in the Chamber of Hewn Stones and decided, "If we let Jesus go on like this, everyone will believe in him, and then the Romans will come and take away both our place and our nation."[125] Fearing both a loss of the status quo and a loss of social status, the religious leaders who *disagreed* on so many issues found common ground in getting rid of Jesus. A man named Caiaphas, who was the high priest that year, then spoke up: "You all know nothing at all! You do not realize that it is better for you that one man dies for the people than the whole nation perish."[126] They all had a vested interest in maintaining their status and income—Jesus had to go. But John tells us that God put those words in Caiaphas's mouth as a prophecy that "Jesus would die for the Jewish nation, and not only for that nation but also for the scattered children of God, to bring them together and make them one."[127] With that, the Sanhedrin voted to place a bounty on Jesus' head. They were out to kill him before he brought anyone else back from the dead.

Beauty

The gift of resurrection and new life deserved a beautiful response. A few weeks after the healing of Lazarus, and six days before the Jewish Passover feast, Jesus went back to Bethany. He went back to the place where the raising of Lazarus occurred, and back to Mary and Martha's house. Imagine Martha for just a moment. In just a few short weeks life had gone from the lowest low to an amazing high. Now, Jesus was coming back for a visit—one she never thought would happen again. Instead of going together with Jesus to visit Lazarus's grave, the four of them would be visiting around a dinner table, just like old times. "Unless," Martha thought, "I decide to throw a big dinner party for Jesus, and Lazarus, in honor of the occasion." A church father, Cyril of Alexandria, supposed Martha picked the day she did because, like today's "Fat Tuesday," "it was a custom not of law but from long usage, for the Jews to have some little merrymaking on the day before the lamb was taken, in order that after the lamb was obtained they might more devote themselves."[128]

Martha decided the occasion warranted such merrymaking—Jesus always loved a good party! Once decided, Martha's hospitality gene kicked into high gear. And once Martha decided she was going to throw a party, it would surely be one of her most extravagant ones—nice in every way. Martha was not just a cook, but a chef among cooks. The best in Bethany. Everyone wanted an invitation to dinner at Martha's house; it was the social event of the season. But a party honoring Jesus and hosted by Lazarus, fresh from the dead, would be a dinner invite of a lifetime. Theodore of Mopsuestia later reflected that many would come to hear Lazarus, "perhaps expecting to hear something extraordinary from him, like somebody who came back to civilization from a strange and remote land."[129] So, Martha sent invitations to all the friends and family who had stuck by them, loved them, and supported them during their four days of grieving: "Come to a party honoring Jesus and celebrating Lazarus!" And of course, everyone would come—if they were present for the mourning, they would surely share in the laughter now!

Martha planned a fitting tribute dinner to the one who had raised her brother from the dead. All Jesus' favorite dishes would be served. She ordered place cards and designated Jesus the "Guest of Honor"[130] and Lazarus the "Host of Honor," placing them prominently at the head of the table. The table was set and fresh flowers cut, a musician played in the courtyard, and a servant was at the front door to wash feet. All things were ready for them to come to her feast. At just the right time, Martha rang the dinner bell, and everyone gathered at the table—a table of thanksgiving. As they saw the lavish banquet, everyone knew it was Martha's way of saying, "Thank you Jesus, for all you've done for us."

What Martha prepared was a thanksgiving (*eucharist* in the Greek) meal. It was a reunion of old friends living and dead; it was a meal for people in communion with Jesus and one another. It was a meal that would have begun, like all Jewish meals do, with the breaking of bread and the words, "Blessed art thou O Lord who brings forth this bread from the ground." Looking at Lazarus, the words "brought forth from the ground" only added to the significance of the moment. And once they began to eat, sister Mary, the impulsive one, began to think in her own love language about how to say "thank you" to Jesus as well. Mary thought back to what life was like for those four horrendous days when her brother was dead. She recalled all the times one of the sisters had said, "We'd trade all we own for one more day with Lazarus. We'd give it all up for one more day as a family." Then and there Mary decided to prove those words true.

Mary got up from the table, went to the back of the house, dug underneath the ground beneath her bed and found the place where she had buried the family valuables. There she pulled out an alabaster jar filled with expensive perfume. How expensive? It was worth a whole year's wages. Before banks, expensive perfume was like a mutual fund—something to invest in, hold, and then sell later at a profitable increase. Just a few weeks ago that perfume was all they had to live on. They had lost the principal breadwinner in Lazarus to provide for them. Their economic future was bleak, worse than unemployment. The one once employed was lost to sickness and the sisters had nowhere else to turn for relief. At that time, the sisters were counting on the perfume to be what they could sell and make ends meet. Jesus had now raised their brother, and the family's finances were still in order. The perfume was now their rainy day/retirement fund.

Mary looked at the beautiful alabaster jar filled with the aroma of sweet perfume, and she thought about Jesus. She thought about the linen strips they had soaked in a perfume before wrapping Lazarus's body. She thought back to the pounds of spices piled upon his body to override the stench of death. Jesus had changed all that. Now Mary's love and devotion to him for what he had done was beyond measure. She had a split-second opportunity to make an impulsive decision: "Will I, or won't I?" Would she pour out their nest egg to honor Jesus? Was what he did really worth it? Or should she be more prudent? Should she be more careful with their finances? Should she be more frugal? All Mary could think to do was to demonstrate extravagant love to the one who had done so much for them.

Walking back to the table, in bold confidence that what she was about to do was right and good, Mary moved toward Jesus with the alabaster jar in her hands. Then uncovering her head and letting down her hair (in a culture that couldn't imagine a woman showing her full head), Mary broke open the jar of expensive perfume and began pouring it on the feet of Jesus. All of sudden, as people saw what was unfolding around the table, the party stopped. One could now hear a pin drop. Everyone watched, not believing what they were witnessing. With all eyes on her, Mary didn't just dab a few drops on Jesus and try to salvage the rest—she poured out the whole bottle. Every last drop. Mary who had sat at the feet of Jesus, Mary who had cried at the feet of Jesus, was now Mary who anointed the feet of Jesus and wiped them with her hair. Few people would do such a thing: show that kind of love, be that kind of vulnerable. The smell of perfume exploded throughout the house. It was extravagant. It was love. It was extravagant love and it was unbridled in its devotion to Jesus.

Judas, the one who would soon betray Jesus, was a guest at the dinner. Judas was indignant at the waste, at the poor stewardship and misuse of funds when there were so many people starving. He looked at Jesus and asked, "How could you let this woman do this? Look at this waste. Look what's taking place here. Do you realize that this could have been sold for a year's wages and the money could have gone to help the poor and the needy?"

In every religious gathering a Judas will be present, questioning motives and telling others how their gifts and talents could be better spent. But Jesus was having none of what Judas was selling. John as the narrator then tells the reader Judas's true motives. Judas didn't speak up because he was into social justice, urban ministry, or spiritual minimalism; Judas said what he did because he kept the books. Cooked the books, actually. Judas was found to take a few kickbacks on the side, and to scrape a little off the top for his personal usage. Jesus stared Judas down and said,

> Leave her alone. This woman has done a beautiful thing. Wherever the gospel is preached, her story will be told. She has prepared me for my burial. Judas, the poor you will always have with you, but you won't always have this opportunity with me.

What Judas saw as wasteful, Jesus saw as beautiful. What Judas saw as careless toward the poor, Jesus saw as caring about his burial. Jesus knew that, like a fine wine, Mary had "guarded" (in the Greek *tereo*) the perfume and "held it in reserve" for this special time and purpose. From Jesus' response, we learn Mary made the right choice when he predicted, "I just received an extravagant gift of love, and every time the gospel is told, this story will be as well."

We know nothing of the dinner conversation, but it must have been merry and must have been meaningful. On this occasion, Jesus may have stepped back and let Lazarus have center stage. He would want to hear Lazarus's account of his four days' journey as much as anyone. Recall that Jesus had met with Moses and Elijah on the Mount of Transfiguration where they discussed Jesus' coming departure (*exodus* in Greek) in Jerusalem brought to fulfillment at the cross.[131] Now, Lazarus was Jesus' scout, his front man, the one who had gone where Jesus was soon journeying. Jesus wanted to hear all about it. In years to come John would write his Revelation and speak about a gift Jesus would give to those who overcame: "To him that overcame, I will also give a white stone with a new name written on it, known only to him who receives it."[132] Lazarus knew what was written on the stone—and was back to testify about it.

Readers of John's Gospel would love to hear all his tales and stories as well, but in all of Scripture Lazarus never speaks. The sisters must have often said as Lazarus's health declined, "He is in God's hands." Now they sat and listened, realizing their brother was an instrument in God's hands—a sword severing soul and spirit and able to pierce through the outer skin of death to the meat and bone of abundant life. Lazarus was an instrument in the hands of God, "the blade of Bethany" telling others of the abundant life beyond the grave. He must have climaxed his adventures beyond the grave with how everything in Hades stopped and became quiet at the bellowing voice of Jesus, and how the next thing he knew he was back among the living simply because Jesus had commanded it. Jesus really was Messiah, a more-than-ever-imagined Messiah.

While the party was going on, a huge crowd gathered outside. They heard that Jesus was there and wanted to hear from him; they also wanted to get a glimpse of Lazarus. It's not every day you meet a man who raises the four days dead, or get to meet a man back again among the living. The crowd began to swell, and Lazarus's fame began to spread as well. Soon the chief priests made plans to kill Lazarus—two for the price of one. It was "on account of Lazarus [that] many of the Jews were going over to Jesus and putting their faith in him."[133] John Chrysostom surmises, "No other miracle of Christ exasperated the Jewish leaders as much as this one. . . . It was so public, and so wonderful, to see a man walking and talking after he had been dead four days. It was so undeniable. In the case of some other miracles they had charged him with breaking the Sabbath and so divert people's minds, but here was nothing to find fault with."[134] The religious leaders feared both that Lazarus would confess Jesus as true Messiah and that Jesus would continue to act as only a true Messiah could. There was now a bounty on both men's heads.

But did Lazarus even care? Death had lost its hold over him. If Jesus had raised him once, he could do it again! Even now Lazarus was living life after life after death. To Lazarus, death had lost its sting.

DEATH BE NOT PROUD

> Death, be not proud, though some have called thee
> Mighty and dreadful, for thou art not so;
> For those whom thou think'st thou dost overthrow
> Die not, poor Death, nor yet canst thou kill me.
> From rest and sleep, which but thy pictures be,
> Much pleasure; then from thee much more must flow,
> And soonest our best men with thee do go,
> Rest of their bones, and soul's delivery.
> Thou art slave to fate, chance, kings, and desperate men,
> And dost with poison, war, and sickness dwell,
> And poppy or charms can make us sleep as well
> And better than thy stroke; why swell'st thou then?
> One short sleep past, we wake eternally
> And death shall be no more; Death, thou shalt die.
>
> —John Donne (1572–1631)[135]

During the days of Jesus' life on earth, he offered up prayers and petitions with fervent cries and tears to the one who could save him from death, and he was heard because of his reverent submission. [8] Son though he was, he learned obedience from what he suffered [9] and, once made perfect, he became the source of eternal salvation for all who obey him [10] and was designated by God to be high priest in the order of Melchizedek.

—HEBREWS 5:7–10

CHAPTER TEN

The Past Is Prologue

Jesus withdrew a stone's throw beyond the disciples, knelt down and prayed, "Father, if you are willing take this cup from me, yet not my will but yours be done." An angel from heaven appeared to him and strengthened him. And being in anguish he prayed more earnestly, and his sweat was like drops of blood falling to the ground.

—LUKE 22:41–44

Never shall I forget that first night in the camp, which has turned my life into one long night, seven times cursed and seven times sealed. Never shall I forget the smoke of the crematorium . . . the smoke that consumed my faith forever. . . . Never shall I forget these moments that murdered my God and my soul, and turned all my dreams to dust.

—*ELIE WIESEL*

JESUS THE MESSIAH MADE his triumphal entry into the royal city of Jerusalem for the final time. Many of the instigators of this royal processional were the same "crowd that was with him when he called Lazarus from the tomb and raised him from the dead."[136] They were continuing to spread the word, and many people who heard of this miraculous sign in nearby Bethany went out to meet Jesus. His followers waved palm branches and lined the parade route with robes and blankets, singing, "Blessed is the one who comes in the name of the Lord." They were ready for the coronation of Jesus as the new king of Israel. But Jesus knew better, and knew the fickle hearts of the masses. So he stopped at the end of the procession to weep (something he seemed to be doing more often these days) over a city and a people who never fully opened their hearts to him. Then it was bedtime. As usual, he camped on the Mount of Olives with his disciples (he probably only grabbed a night's sleep on the couch at Lazarus's house when all the disciples were not with him). That same night, the Pharisees were saying to each other, "See this is getting us nowhere. Look how the whole world has gone after him!"[137] Jesus was on a collision course, a final confrontation, with dark power.

The next day Jesus arose early from his camp on the hillside of the Mount of Olives and made his way down through the Kidron Valley. There he soaked in the sight of the Beautiful Gate and the temple completed by Herod the Great. Entering inside, Jesus discovered the area God prescribed be built for gentile prayer was now filled with moneychangers and merchants selling animals for sacrifices. A place designed as a house of prayer for foreigners was now filled with the clanking of coins and the bleating of sheep. There was no place for outsiders to pray or for foreign travelers coming from great distances to connect with Yahweh—the One God of Israel. Jesus made a whip from a few scattered cords and began to crack it on the stone pavement to make sure it worked. His apostles began to both grin and cringe, realizing what would happen next. In a flash, Jesus sprang into action and drove the animals out the gate called "Beautiful" and into the valley below. The owners, who stood to secure a huge profit that day, were now chasing the spooked sheep in the valley below. The next thing anyone knew, the sound of the moneychangers' small wooden tables being toppled on stone pavement boomed and then the clanking of coins bounding across the granite floors followed. The commotion of coins clanking on the stone pavement and the hooves of sheep scampering about focused everyone's attention upon the moment. Jesus had created quite a scene. And people everywhere could hear Jesus shouting, "This house shall be a place of prayer for everyone—not a den for robbers." Some thought they even heard him call the temple "my Father's house."

No one doubted what Jesus did was right and true, but religious leaders did inquire as to why Jesus felt he had the authority to do it. He countered their question not with another question, as he usually did, but with

an odd saying: "Destroy this house and I will build it again in three days."
It had taken Herod the Great nearly forty-six years to build the magnificent
structure that was now the crown jewel of the Middle East. Jesus planned
to see it toppled and rebuilt in the length of a holiday weekend. Only later
did his disciples understand that his "three days" reference was concerning
his physical body. Jesus knew there was one place on earth where God's
presence resided more fully than even the holy of holies inside that temple!
All the fullness of God was pleased to dwell in him.

Jesus stayed at the temple throughout the day to teach and instruct the
large crowds gathering each day of the Passover celebration. But the religious leaders retired to the backrooms, to once again discuss terminating
Jesus before he cost them everything they had worked so hard to obtain. Instead of placing another bounty on Jesus' head, or hoping someone would
get their hints and do the deed, they began plotting Jesus' assassination
themselves. They had all the contacts, they had money, they had influence,
and they had access to shady people who did shady things—"fixers" to help
keep the religious system working. Jesus' presence threatened everything:
their way of life, their cozy relationship with Rome, and their connection to
power through the unholy alliances they had made.

These venerated rulers of Jerusalem decided the best way to take
down Jesus was to trap him in his own words, and then use any misspeak
to convict. Earlier they brought a solitary woman caught in adultery (what
happened to it taking "two to tango"?) and asked Jesus if they should stone
her. Throwing stones to kill a wayward woman might be what the Old
Testament Law of Moses said to do, but this ancient Jewish code violated
modern Roman Law, which did not consider sexual sin a capital offense.
Adultery might have been a capital offense when Israel was its own ruler,
but under Roman rule the Romans made the laws, and adultery was not an
offense punishable by death. The Jews were certain Jesus would pick a side
in judging the woman: God's law or Rome's law. And once Jesus did, they
could then spring their trap. If Jesus sided with the Romans, they would
convict him for opposing God's law; if he sided with God's law, then they
would turn him in to the Romans. Either way they had him! But instead,
Jesus bent over and drew in the dirt. Then standing erect he announced,
"The one with no sin should cast the first stone." Then he bent over to draw
in the dirt a bit more. Now the shoe was on each leader's foot, and they all
dropped rocks and went their way.

Now, another leader came to Jesus asking, "Is it lawful to pay taxes to Caesar or not?" They questioned how any self-respecting Jew could pay taxes in tribute to an emperor who considered himself a god, or the son of god, to be worshiped. Yet how in a world dominated by Rome could one avoid paying the tax either? Surely Jesus would take a side (either side) and then they could convict him of being in cahoots with Rome (if he said pay it) or turn Jesus in to the Romans (for insurrection) if he counseled refusal to pay taxes. Either way they figured to trap Jesus in his own words and use them to condemn him. Instead, Jesus called for a coin. "Whose face is this on the coinage? Whose likeness is this?" he asked. When the people responded, "Caesar's," he then coolly flipped the coin back to the one who gave it and replied, "Then render to Caesar the things that belong to Caesar, but since your life is created in God's image, give your life to God."

At this the leaders went away and gave up the futile quest of entrapping Jesus in his own words. Next, the leaders gathered the biggest guns in their arsenal: summoning the Jewish congress into secret session at the high priest's palace to consider what to do with the one now clearly seen as the people's messiah. The Jewish leaders knew any messiah they embraced would be seen by Rome as a threat to the emperor—and would result in brutality and bloodshed for the people of Jerusalem. They had seen it before with the Maccabean revolt and would opt for maintaining their own limited power under Roman rule, rather than suffering for the outlandish claims to messiahship made by a carpenter from Nazareth. When the grumbling and the speeches in the Sanhedrin began to draw down, the Chief Priest Caiaphas arose. A few weeks earlier, after the raising of Lazarus in Bethany, he had said these words:

> You men know nothing at all! You do not realize that it is better for
> you that one man die for the people rather than the whole nation
> perish. (John 11:50)

His words then were both heartless and prophetic, as Caiaphas prophesied that Jesus would die for the Jewish nation, and not only for the nation but for all those scattered children of God awaiting the Lord's redemption. This time he doubled down on his language by activating the plot "to arrest Jesus in some sly way and kill him, 'But not during the Feast,' he added, 'or there may be a riot among the people.'"[138] So from that moment on, the religious leaders of all Israel united under the common cause of eradicating Jesus from the earth—but not during Passover, lest the people be incensed and riot.

On Thursday Jesus arranged for a special dinner with his disciples. A friend had a guest room, an upper room, that was all set and prepared for them to celebrate Passover, even if it was bit early. Throughout the day, Jesus watched as the disciples sniped at one another and jockeyed for positions, and for pecking order, among the twelve. This was precipitated by the actions of Mrs. Zebedee, the mother of James and John. She had come to Jesus in an end run to secure the best positions for her boys in Jesus' cabinet—assuming Jesus would soon drive out the Romans and set up his own throne. All the apostles assumed that Jesus would be that kind of messiah, a king with a kingdom, an army and royal advisors. They were each putting in bids for the best spots in the new king's cabinet. Jesus had warned them not long ago that he had come to be a servant, not to be served, and to give his life on behalf of others.[139] But they did not understand what he was saying and craved power and influence—*We deserve something after three years of service*, each one thought. At dinner that night the feast was prepared, but the servant to wash feet was not at his basin and towel. Everyone sat to eat with smelly feet, until Jesus arose from the head of the table, took off his robe, and placed a towel around his waist. Jesus then went from apostle to apostle and washed all twenty-four feet. When he was done, he returned to the head of the table and asked, "Do you understand what I have done for you? You like to call me 'Teacher' and 'Lord,' and in both cases you are right." Jesus then bid his disciples, "If I your teacher and Lord have washed your feet, you also should wash one another's feet. I have set you an example that you should do as I have done for you. . . . Now that you know what you ought to do, you will be blessed if you do it."[140]

After everyone's feet were clean, Jesus wanted to commemorate a special evening. He took bread and held in high above his head. He prayed, "Blessed art thou O Lord who brings forth this bread from the ground." He broke the bread in half and gave it to his apostles, saying, "This bread represents my body that is given for you. As often as you eat it, do so in remembrance of me." The disciples thought back to the feeding of the five thousand, the feeding of the four thousand, and the time he called himself "the Bread of Life." After that, Jesus took a glass of wine and held it up, saying, "This cup is a new covenant in my blood, which is poured out for you." Looking at his dear friends he then added, "I tell you the truth, I will not drink again of the fruit of the vine until that day when I drink it anew in the kingdom of God."[141] After that, they sang a hymn and left for the Mount of Olives—all except Judas.

Early in the Passover meal, Judas ultimately decided to be the accomplice who would betray Jesus. Hiring him to do the deed took thirty pieces of silver. The religious leaders wanted to avoid doing anything during Passover, but the best laid plans of the high priest changed when a willing accomplice, a fall-guy, arrived on the scene. In Judas of Iscariot they had found their man. So they struck while the iron was hot. Judas was considered trustworthy among the apostolic band, the keeper of the moneybags for the group. Yet, he was a crook. He pretended to care for the poor at the dinner for Jesus and Lazarus where Mary had shown extravagant love—but what motivated his condemnation of Mary was self-interest. Judas's thirst for money now led him to concoct a sting where the authorities could arrest Jesus quietly under the cover of night. Jesus was all about the daylight, and Judas was about the night—deeds done in secret. Judas knew how a typical day would go for Jesus while in Jerusalem. Jesus would end his day (as he always did) praying in the garden of Gethsemane just outside Jerusalem on the Mount of Olives. The people would not be around to riot, and the apostles would come ill-prepared to defend their master. Jesus could be arrested, tried, and executed before most people would hear the news—as no newspapers were delivered on the Sabbath.

Judas's strategy was quickly adopted by the chief priest and the rest of the Sanhedrin. It had been a long time since this group had agreed upon anything—but they united around the eradication of the Jesus-threat. The details were set, and the plan was soon in motion. Jesus' arrest in Gethsemane on a Thursday night played out like a Shakespearean tragedy—betrayed by a kiss from his trusted friend. Where Shakespeare's Julius Caesar would later say, "Et tu Brute?" Jesus would simply ask, "Judas, do you now betray me with a kiss?"[142] Peter put up a fight, grabbing one of their only swords and taking the ear off a servant named Malchus. But Jesus picked up the ear and put it back as if nothing had happened. Then he turned and asked the leaders, "Why here? Why now?" Jesus went on to ask if they really thought he was leading a rebellion where swords and clubs were necessary. He reminded them, "Every day I was with you in the temple courts, and you did not lay a hand on me. But this is your hour—when darkness reigns."[143] Jesus asked that his followers be spared, and with that the apostolic band that was once ready to die with Jesus scattered like a covey of quail at the first crack of shotgun fire. One of his followers was captured but broke loose to flee home naked—it was that bad. Jesus was abandoned and alone—the worst kind of quarantine mankind has ever experienced. The foxes had come, the sheep had scattered, and the Great Shepherd was left to die for his sheep. Bound like a lamb being led to the slaughter, Jesus was led to Caiaphas's house for a midnight kangaroo court and a swift indictment. It was night, the darkest night the world had ever known.

The Sanhedrin secretly gathered again in the family palace of Annas and Caiaphas (the high priestly family) to begin "legal proceedings" that were illegal in Israel. Jewish law forbade trials without due process, and evening trials were specifically condemned by the Talmud. Mob rule had quickly set in as the religious leaders told themselves they were acting in the best interest of all Israel. They began peppering Jesus with questions about his disciples and his teachings, hoping to trap him in something he would say. But Jesus stood on his past record, stating, "I always taught in synagogues or at the temple, where all Jews come together. I said nothing in secret. Why question me? Ask those who heard me. Surely they know what I said." For that comment, one of the nearby officials struck Jesus in the face and said, "Is this the way you answer the high priest?" Jesus merely turned the other cheek and stated, "If I said something wrong tell me. If I spoke the truth why did you strike me?"[144] Soon the leaders saw they were getting nowhere in their attempt to indict Jesus, so they fabricated witnesses accusing Jesus of opposing the temple and opposing the emperor. They then condemned Jesus in short order and sent him over to the Roman governor, Pilate, in Antonio's Fortress. The name "Pilate" was supposed to mean "pillar," but this supposed leader first tried to pass the buck by sending Jesus to Herod Antipas, who was in town for Passover as well. Antipas was the political puppet of Rome that Jesus had nicknamed "that fox." Antipas was clever like a fox, and after questioning Jesus sent the supposed messiah back to Pilate in the clothing of a king so that both leaders might get a good laugh at Jesus' expense. Pilate then caved to the will of an angry mob (even over his wife's strong warnings) and released an insurrectionist named Barabbas while condemning Jesus to the cruelest of all deaths—execution on a cross.

Jesus was sent to the lower recesses of Antonio's Fortress, where the flagellum was used to savagely whip him thirty-nine times—he absorbed the pain, leaving the skin of his back shredded and bleeding. The soldiers then played the "King's Game," most likely dressing Jesus again in the royal clothes sent by Herod and placing a crown of thorns upon his head in place of a laurel. They smashed it into his skull, and Jesus absorbed the blows as soldiers looked on and as blood ran down Jesus' brow. They then led him through the Via Delarosa, the way of the cross, until Jesus reached the place called "the Skull." It was here at this intimidating location, on a high bluff, that he was crucified between two thieves. Nailing Jesus' hands to the cross beam he had carried with a little help from Simon of Cyrene, the soldiers then crossed his feet on the main beam and used a single nail to secure him there. Hoisting the cross with Jesus nailed to it into the air, the soldiers dropped it down into a hole with a loud thud. Simultaneous to the thud, they heard the shriek of excruciating pain as the impact tore into the flesh of Jesus. It was 9:00 a.m. on Friday morning when the agony began, and Jesus uttered his first words from his cross-shaped pulpit only seconds afterwards. As he was being lifted up and cruelly dropped into place, Jesus uttered this heartfelt prayer: "Father, forgive them for they do not know what they are doing."

Over the course of the next six hours Jesus would speak a total of seven times. Jesus' first words were of forgiveness. He followed those later with words of assurance for a thief sharing Calvary's crosses with him: "Surely today you will be with me in Paradise." Next Jesus turned his attention towards his mother and his dear friend John the apostle, saying, "Woman, behold your new son; and son, behold your new mother." Jesus and his mother were physically separated at that moment with no way to touch one another in this last moment together, but Jesus assured her of his undying devotion. From then on, John was the one who cared for Mary until her dying days. Jesus' first three sayings from the cross each dealt with righting relationships, and they reveal him responding with unimaginable love right up to the bitter end.

Jesus' final three sayings, "I thirst," "It is finished," and "Into your hands I commit my Spirit," would later each announce Jesus' resolve and readiness to complete the task before him. In the garden of Gethsemane just the night before, Jesus had on three occasions begged his Father to "take this cup far away from me—yet not what I want, but what you want be done." The cup Jesus begged not to drink in the garden was not the cup of death or suffering, for Jesus had spoken openly about his willingness to suffer and die. The contents of the cup had to be something else. Inside was the bitterest of medicines that Jesus begged and pleaded not to taste—the undiluted sin of the entire world. This was the ultimate virus, and Jesus was bid by his Father to drink in and take upon himself all the viral consequences of sin run rampant throughout the world. The contents would separate the Father and the Son for the first time in all of history. Yesterday, Jesus had begged his Father not to drink it, but now from the cross, knowing what had to be done, Jesus announced in a loud voice, "I am thirsty!" It was Jesus' way of saying, "Bring it on!" As the sky turned dark and the earth began to tremble beneath onlookers' feet, Jesus then announced he had completed the task before him with two short utterances. The first announced the completion of his task: "It is finished." Then Jesus bowed his head and gave up his spirit, saying, "Into your hands, I return my breath."

It was in between sayings one through three and sayings five through seven that Jesus went through what King David rightly called "the valley of the shadow of death."[145] The last time the world had been this dark was the moment before his Father had spoken, "Let there be light," ushering light into a dark and chaotic cosmos. The hatred and disgrace heaped upon Jesus by the people of Jerusalem and the religious leaders brought him to the same place King David had been a thousand years earlier. The same words David had spoken in the depths of his grief over Absalom now became the only words Jesus could summon to explain the dark place where he found himself.

Jesus as the "word made flesh" was searching for the right words to adequately describe his own feelings of utter abandonment. Abandoned by the crowds, who quickly turned on him after a triumphal welcome. Abandoned by disciples who claimed they'd die for him, but scurried before the rooster crowed. But most painful of all by far, Jesus was abandoned by his Father, who had always been there before. This hurt the most, for the God whose very nature could not abandon faithfulness had abandoned him to a cross. Made to die in quarantine, far away from his Father, Jesus was a man of sorrow familiar with every grief. Jesus drank the bitter cup of all the unfaithful deeds ever done; and he drank it alone.

At this moment Jesus absorbed in himself the viral sin that had infected the entire cosmos. He was in isolation from his Father.

In the midst of his agony on the cross, Jesus summoned all his strength to rise up on the cross beam and take in a large gasp of air. Oxygenated, Jesus shouted with all his might words that had echoed through the hills and valleys around Jerusalem for over a millennium:

> *Eloi, Eloi, lama sabachthani*—My God, my God, why have you forsaken me?

Words first uttered by a father who had lost a beloved son now became the utterance of a beloved Son abandoned by his Father.

Yet no sooner had Jesus uttered these words of forsakenness than his Father gave him a new perspective. It hit him like a lightning bolt and allowed him to see the divine plan his Father had put into motion weeks earlier to help him through this very moment. Jesus' mind was drawn back to the arrival of the messenger from Bethany, the four days of isolation, and the encounter he faced in the death of his best friend. In that instant, the Lazarus story made sense of his current life-and-death moment in ways unimaginable. He now understood what his time in spiritual isolation and quarantine was all about and why his Father allowed him to absorb the world's grief so completely.

WHEN I SURVEY THE WONDROUS CROSS

When I survey the wondrous cross
Oh which the Prince of glory died
My richest gain I count but loss
And pour contempt on all my pride
Forbid it, Lord, that I should boast,
Save in the death of Christ my God
All the vain things that charm me most,
I sacrifice them to His blood
See from his head, his hands, his feet,
Sorrow and love flow mingled down!
Did e'er such love and sorrow meet,
Or thorns compose so rich a crown?
Were the whole realm of nature mine,
That were a present far too small,
Love so amazing, so divine,
Demands my soul, my life, my all.

—Isaac Watts (1674–1748)[146]

PART TWO

Do not be amazed at this, for a time is coming when all who are in their graves will hear his voice and come out—those who have done what is good will rise to live, and those who have done what is evil will rise to be condemned.

—JOHN 5:28–29

CHAPTER ELEVEN

Walking in Another's Moccasins:
Roles of Father and Son

I do not have anything to offer my readers except my conviction that when pain is to be borne, a little courage helps more than much knowledge, a little human sympathy more than much courage, and the least tincture of the love of God more than all.

—C. S. LEWIS

To come to pleasure you have not, you must go by a way in which you enjoy not.

—SAINT JOHN OF THE CROSS

JESUS ABSORBED THE BETRAYAL of Judas, the abandonment of his apostles, the false accusation of the religious leaders, and the blows of the soldiers. He absorbed the shame of the cross and the agony of carrying it. Jesus absorbed the pain of the nails shooting through his hands and feet and the violent act of dropping him into place. He absorbed the taunting of prisoners and the brutality of callous soldiers. He absorbed the taunts of the religious leaders and the tears of his mother and friends as they stood near the cross. But there was one more grief to absorb; it would be the painfullest of all.

Jesus used all his energy to raise himself up on the cross to draw a deep breath. In so doing he inhaled the stale air filled with the echoing cry David uttered over a thousand years earlier. It had bounced around the canyon walls with nothing to absorb it . . . until now. Now those words of David's were his words, and he bellowed them out from his cross shaped podium: "*Eloi, Eloi, lama sabachthani*—My God, my God, why have you forsaken me?"

But as soon as he asked his question, he knew his answer. His question asked at Calvary, God had already answered for him in Bethany.

Jesus' mind was drawn back to the arrival of the messenger from Bethany, the two-day wait, and the encounter he faced in the death of his best friend. In that instant, the Lazarus story made sense of his present suffering in ways unimaginable as it was unfolding. He now understood what his time in the spiritual isolation and quarantine was all about and how his Father had used grief to help him absorb life lessons in Bethany that would prepare him for this moment at Calvary. It was now clear to Jesus that in Bethany, God the Father had allowed him to play the "Fatherly" role in the Lazarus episode. Jesus had walked a few days in his Father's moccasins. In other words, the role his Father was now playing for him at the cross, he had just played for Lazarus in Bethany.

JESUS CAST IN THE ROLE OF THE "FATHER"

From the cross he now understood why his Father made him wait two days and passively absorb all the grief and pain in isolation before returning to Bethany on the "third day." His Father wanted Jesus to feel towards Lazarus what the Father was feeling for him now. Jesus harkened back to those three days he had to social distance himself from Bethany and wait, when all he wanted to do was be present to absorb the grief of those he loved. He thought about how agonizing the isolation had been and how badly he'd wanted to drop everything and go running to Lazarus and the sisters. Now Jesus realized that his Father was experiencing those same feelings towards him. All his Father wanted to do was come running with ten thousand angels, ready to destroy the world and set him free. But instead, his Father was distant at the moment, not because he wanted to be—but because he had to do so. This isolation between Father and Son was part of the cure—not to flatten the curve of sin but to obliterate it for good. The Father was waiting, not because of better things to do, but because the fullness of time had not yet arrived. Jesus remembered how difficult it was to answer Martha and Mary's telegram prayer with "No, not yet" and recognized the Father had answered his prayers in Gethsemane the same way. "Let this cup pass from me" was his desperate telegram of prayer—and his Father too had said, "No, not yet."

Oddly, perhaps, Jesus knew that at the same instant the Father was saying "Not yet" to his beloved Son, the Father was also still engaged in answering the prayers of the righteous who prayed to him day and night. Just as Jesus kept working for two days at the Jordan while his heart was in Bethany, his Father was still working answering the prayers of the world even while his Son hung in agony. He remembered the time at the Jordan, listening to stories, healing the sick, casting out demons, and feeding the hungry—all the while having his heart focused upon Lazarus and Bethany. He began to realize the Father was now doing the same. The Father was now sitting in his own isolation, quarantined from his son, tying his own hands from acting on behalf of his only Son.

God the Father in spiritual isolation; who could have imagined? Sacred distancing. The One who is omnipresent chose to hide himself from his Son. The One all-powerful did not use power to aid his own Son. A Father-God who was all-powerful and all-loving did not help his only begotten Son in his greatest hour of need. Who would have thought?

Jesus thought about the sucker punch to the gut that the death of Lazarus had been for him—and how his own death would inflict deep pathos upon his Father. Jesus had once said, "Lazarus is dead, and for your sakes I am glad." Similarly, now Jesus was hanging, dying on a cross, and his Father was glad, for the sake of the world. Jesus was the cure for the pandemic of sin, and his Father had to let the cure run its course. Jesus had never hurt like he did that day in Bethany, and he had never cried as he did at that moment either. Perhaps the darkness over the land and the earthquake that occurred as Jesus hung on the cross were creation's manifestations of the grief being absorbed by his Father. God the Father was in anguish as he watched his beloved Son die in isolation upon a cruel cross.

Flashing forward, Jesus knew what was ahead for his Father—because it had unfolded already for him. After three days, the Father would begin to take action just as he had finally been allowed to do. The Father would arrive at the stone sealed tomb and announce to all those below in Hades that the great "I AM" had come to bring Resurrection and Life. Those long awaiting this good news from beyond the grave[147] would rejoice and realize that metamorphosis into new life and new creation was almost complete. Just as Jesus had overcome sin and death for Lazarus, now his Father would announce he was doing so for all humanity through the raising of Jesus from the dead. Jesus remembered getting to tell Martha, "Your brother will rise again," and could only imagine the joy his Father would receive in proclaiming such things about him.

Jesus flashed forward to a tomb, carved from a cave, with a stone across the entrance. He recalled saying, "Take the stone away," only to have Martha protest. This time, Jesus concluded, "No angel will protest when my Father says, 'Roll away the stone.'" Jesus remembered shouting in a loud voice and Lazarus coming out. He then looked forward to the voice awaiting him, in a few short days, when his time of resurrection would come. Lazarus had recognized Jesus' voice and come forth; it was probably the favorite moment of Jesus' time upon the earth. Now Jesus awaited the Voice that had spoken the world into creation, bidding Jesus return as Lazarus had done. He knew his would be an even better reunion. He looked forward to that voice then telling angels to remove the grave clothes and give him the new clothes needed for his resurrected body.

He thought about the meal with Martha, Mary, and Lazarus and how fun it was to celebrate new life. Jesus then fast-forwarded to the celebration in heaven that would surpass it, when Jesus returned to his home. He thought about the heavenly banquet to come, when the Father would be host and he would sit as guest of honor—just as Lazarus had done. He looked forward to the great feast, the toasts, and the celebration that would ensue.

God his Father had given him grief to absorb in Bethany so that he would understand his moment now at Golgatha. Wisdom is seeing present life situations from the perspective of God the Father. Jesus realized through Lazarus and Bethany, the Father had given him the wisdom to handle what he was now experiencing. Through the window of Bethany, he now understood how to process the feelings of abandonment pressing upon him at the cross.

Where was God the Father? Was he still all-powerful? Was he still all-loving? Why did bad things happen to a good man like Lazarus? Where was the Father at the moment of need?

He was where Jesus the Son had been when Martha and Mary asked the same questions about abandonment and isolation, sickness and death. In spiritual isolation. The Father was waiting for the moment when resurrection, life, and new creation could be revealed. Jesus now knew why he felt forsaken. He felt what Lazarus, Martha, and Mary had felt towards him. He felt abandoned and isolated, as they had felt abandoned—yet he also knew the rest of the story. He simply had to absorb what they could not—there was no other way.

Jesus knew the "why" to this story as well. God loved him, and everything happening now would bring glory to the Father, and to his Son. And through the Son, resurrection and life would now be available to everyone.

LAZARUS CAST IN THE "JESUS" ROLE

From the cross Jesus also realized Lazarus had played the suffering role he, Jesus, now played at the cross. In no way did Lazarus die for the salvation of mankind. But Lazarus was a window through which Jesus could see himself, a lower picture of a higher reality. Lazarus was infected with a virus that brought death. But Jesus had willingly chosen to drink the cup filled with every virus, every cancer, every cruel human action ever perpetrated by the human race. In Lazarus, Jesus caught a glimpse of his own present reality—infected with sin and left to die. Jesus had been watching as a spectator while his friend walked through the valley of the shadow of death; now Jesus traveled behind. Lazarus served as a signpost for John's Gospel, but also for Jesus personally—offering the Savior of the World a glimpse into the incredible isolation awaiting him at his own passion.

Lazarus was Jesus' closest friend, the one Jesus could have easily called "beloved." Yet not even that designation kept Lazarus well when sickness came calling. Jesus recalled multiple occasions when his Father had acknowledged him as his "beloved"—the only begotten one that the Father loved. Once, at Jesus' baptism, a voice from heaven announced this deepest of relationships, saying, "You are my Son, whom I love; with you I am well pleased."[148] Later at the Transfiguration, a fatherly voice thundered from the clouds, announcing, "This is my Son, whom I love; listen to him!"[149] Yet being the beloved of the Father did not spare Jesus from taking upon himself sin and death. Jesus now fully realized that Lazarus, his beloved friend, played the role of "beloved one" condemned to die by the workings of the Evil One. Lazarus as his understudy opened a window into the viral contagion of sin now heaped upon him.

As Jesus' most beloved friend, Lazarus experienced firsthand the feeling of betrayal when Jesus did not arrive to help as he could. Now Jesus was feeling betrayed as well. Lazarus kept calling out for Jesus, but absence and spiritual isolation were the only responses. Now Jesus' own calls were going unanswered instead. As Lazarus slipped into death's sleep, his final cry of abandonment was now Jesus' own. What Lazarus once felt in Jesus' own absence was now Jesus' own feeling at the hand of his Father.

Jesus knew better than anyone the harsh reality sin was in the world. He saw how his friend Lazarus bore in his body the infection of sin, the wages of sin and death brought on by sin. Jesus watched as Lazarus experienced the full consequences of his *own* sin, which led to his illness, his death, and his separation from the land of the living. Lazarus's sickness was a direct result of the fall and was a tool of the enemy, Satan. The consequences of the actions of the first Adam, and all his descendants, were visited upon Lazarus. Now Jesus, from the cross, was doing something about it. On the cross, Jesus drank the viral contagion of sin and death and absorbed the grief he had prayed only a night before to let pass from him. When Jesus cried out from the cross, "I am thirsty!" it was with the love of his friends in mind that he took on the full wages of their sin.

Through Lazarus, Jesus realized his Father had provided him with a guide for his journey unto death. Earlier, his Father had sent Moses and Elijah to discuss "exodus" plans with him in a transfiguration atop Mount Tabor. Lazarus, who had experienced the full force of death and all the hardships associated with it, was now made available to talk with Jesus about it. Moses and Elijah had joined Jesus on a mountain, but Lazarus was Jesus' "mentor" to journey with him through the valley of the shadow of death.

Jesus missed Lazarus's funeral—he was still in his Father's spiritual isolation. Jesus likewise missed the family burial, but did get to see Lazarus in his funeral clothes. He saw the tomb, the stone over the entrance, and mourners surrounding it. Jesus caught a sniff of the spices covering over the stench of death, before they became the sweet aroma of life again. While Jesus was awaiting his clearance from the Father to travel to Bethany, Lazarus was given his travel papers and descended into Hades to await a resurrection—only to be summoned to return to life again. Lazarus made all the steps from death to the grave to the waiting place that Jesus would soon make. Jesus would later be called "the first-fruit from among the dead" because he would rise in a glorious new body never to die again. But Lazarus was Jesus' scout who traveled a similar course ahead of his friend and Lord.

Jesus thought of that day Lazarus was raised. The sisters were so certain there was no possibility left, the townspeople were down on Jesus for his late arrival, and all hope seemed lost. But then Jesus cried out, "Lazarus, come forth," and the sounds of new creation began to be heard. Loosening the cloth from his friend's face, Jesus would never forget that smile as Lazarus showed him the goodness of the Lord in the land of the living. Then Lazarus explained so simply, "I heard your voice call for me, and so I got up and came." As soon as Lazarus got free of the grave clothes and changed into fresh new ones, all Lazarus wanted to do was be—be with those he loved. And everyone just wanted to hang on to him—not let him go again (as Mary would soon do to Jesus as well). Lazarus was the same old man but an entirely new man at the same time. There was a joy and a power in him not present before. Living his old life as a new creation had made all things new for him too.

From that day forward, Jesus had seen himself in Lazarus as in no one else. Lazarus had, in a way, shared in Christ's sufferings and become like him in death. He had experienced the full force of the Evil One's viral contagion of sin and death, but he had also experienced the greater power of the resurrection and seemed to know Christ through his suffering in a way others could not yet understand.[150] Jesus would later reveal the reason: "Blessed and holy are those who have part in the first resurrection. The second death has no power over them, but they will be priests of God and Christ and will reign with him for a thousand years."[151]

ALL CREATURES OF OUR GOD AND KING

> And thou most kind and gentle Death,
> Waiting to hush our latest breath,
> O praise Him! Alleluia!
> Thou leadest home the child of God,
> And Christ our Lord the way hath trod.
> O praise Him, O praise Him.

> Let all things their Creator bless,
> And worship Him in humbleness.
> O praise Him! Alleluia!
> Praise, praise the Father, praise the Son,
> And praise the Spirit, three in One!
> O praise Him! O praise Him!

> —Saint Francis of Assisi (c. 1181–1226)[152]

CHAPTER TWELVE

Mary and Martha Cast in the "Church" Role

I am deeply convinced that there is a ministry in which our leaving creates space for God's spirit and in which, by our absence, God can become present in a new way. There is an enormous difference between an absence after a visit and an absence which is the result of not coming at all. Without a coming there can be no leaving, and without a presence absence is only emptiness and not the way to a greater intimacy with God through the Spirit.

—HENRY NOUWEN

Surely He has borne our griefs, and carried our sorrows; yet we esteemed Him stricken, smitten by God, and afflicted.

—ISA 53:4

JESUS LOOKED FROM THE cross further into the future and realized that his friends who were like family, Mary and Martha, opened a window into the world to come as well. They represented all who would follow after Jesus and comprise his church. Martha would champion the rational, thinking, cerebral side of the body of Christ. Mary would make up the emotive and highly emotional side of things. The church as the great family of God would be diminished and boring if both were not present. Jesus could not imagine a stay at the Lazarus home without both sisters being present, nor could he imagine a church without the gifts of each included as well. How diminished his visits would have been without the preparation, planning, and near perfection Martha seemed to bring to everything she touched! She was, in a good and gracious way, about total quality. But how boring things would have soon become without Mary there to bring laughter, love, and legitimacy to the relational side of life. He saw in these two sisters a model for the church.

Each sister desired as close to perpetual communion with Jesus as could be had on this earth. They welcomed him into their home regularly and with great fanfare and celebration. Signs, notes, and gestures all let him know he had a place in their hearts and a ready welcome mat into their home. They were proud to be known as "the place where Jesus was always welcome" and loved it when Jesus spoke about experiencing "more love at their house than anywhere else on earth." Jesus hoped one day people would say the same about his church.

Lazarus, Martha, and Mary were about as different as three siblings could be, but their love for Jesus seemed to have drawn them together into sweet fellowship. The differences in personality that once drove the two others almost crazy were now embraced, even laughed at, as a unique addition to the family system that would be missed if ever taken away. This was what Jesus had prayed to the Father for in his high priestly prayer,[153] that through differences God would make his family *one*.

Jesus thought about the day sin's viral contagion brought Lazarus to his knees and swiftly into bed. He knew how the sisters had stepped forward to care for their brother, exactly as he had taught them. With no thought to their own condition they accompanied their brother, absorbing his pain and entering fully into his care. They sat with him 'round the clock and fed, bathed, and read to him. They brought a cup of cold water in Jesus' name and applied a damp rag to his forehead while reciting favorites from the psalter. Like later healthcare professionals, they exhausted themselves in Lazarus's care and discovered the "food others knew nothing about" that Jesus had mentioned to the disciples as he sat with a woman at a well.[154] Jesus was proud of the quality care the sisters had shown, and he knew no other moment had revealed to them their great capacity to love as this moment had done. Jesus had left instructions that his church would accompany the sick, offer a cup of cold water, and attend to those in death—and the sisters modeled this for future followers. Everyone could tell they were his followers by the way they loved—it testified of him.

As proud as Jesus was of all the sisters' care, perhaps nothing they did pleased him like the telegram of prayer they sent. They actually sent it! So many followers would have made excuses for not sending it: "Jesus is too busy," "We are too busy to stop and send it," "Jesus knows already, so why tell him?" or "Jesus got the world going but now this is in the hands of Providence." Jesus heard each prayer offered, but what many disciples fail to recognize is that he also knows of every prayer withheld. It's a slap in the face when the telegram goes unsent and a source of great joy when Jesus is trusted enough to be contacted. The sisters' message was heartfelt, crafted in hope, and sent with both the warmth of familial love and the intimacy of friendship love. Their telegram of intercession made their case to Jesus as big brother and friend and placed Lazarus squarely into Jesus' hands. The sisters left Lazarus to the goodness of Jesus. This is why Jesus was able to say, "God will be glorified through this." Jesus wondered again from the cross what he had queried after telling the parable of the widow and the wicked judge—"Will my church pray and never give up?" And when I return one day, "Will I find such faith on the earth?"[155]

Jesus thought again about his three-day absence and how hard it had been on him to stay put. He then thought about the sisters and what his absence had stirred in them on three levels: 1) it caused them to doubt the effectiveness of their telegram of intercession, 2) it caused them to doubt the loving relationship they had with Jesus, and 3) it caused them to doubt whether Jesus would ever return at all. His Father surely knew that this would be the immediate reaction—doubt the instrument, doubt the relationship, doubt the return—but the Father had insisted on this ministry of absence anyway. Jesus recognized that the absence created in the sisters something of unmistakable value: *longing*. His absence from them in the body produced the positive affect of "longing for God's presence and for God's reign and rule." The sisters, through his absence, had become more desperate for God than at any time he knew them. There was a ministry in his absence after all!

The sisters had begged the Father to send the ministering presence of Jesus and the power of the Holy Spirit within him. They asked Jesus to do a mighty work in their home, their community, and their village for the glory of God alone. Jesus knew the future followers who made up his church would experience a similar absence of Jesus and think it "abandonment."

However, it was the spiritual isolation that genuinely seemed to open wider the portals of the human heart to prayer. He hoped they would pray on, and trust in his love that never fails—and not give up. And he hoped he'd hear the same words from his church that he had heard so often from the sisters, "*Marana tha!*"[156]—"Come, Lord Jesus!"

Jesus thought about how the sisters had come out of the village to meet him outside the city. He smiled when he thought of how glad he was to see them. And it warmed his heart to realize how their frustrations about his long delay in returning seemed to wash away at the first glimpse of his presence. All the questions the sisters thought they'd want to ask him seemed trivial and insignificant once he had arrived. Jesus smiled as he thought about the sisters who thought they knew him better than anyone. They had no idea of the extent of his glory and power, but Mary came closest when she fell at his feet and worshiped. Jesus thought about the day to come when the trumpet would sound, and all the dead in him would rise first. He dreamed about that day when those he had never met face to face (living and dead) would go out to meet him in the air and see him face to face for the first time. He imagined the grand processional as the church led him into the New Jerusalem as the sisters had led him into Bethany. He recognized that Martha and Mary represented all those to come who would usher him into the Holy City that came down from the heaven. He looked forward to the day when they would enter rejoicing and singing the new "Song of Moses and the Lamb."

Jesus considered how this event had given the sisters the language of death, burial, and resurrection for the first time as well. Jesus thought back to Martha's insistence that death and burial would be the end of Lazarus's story. She begged him not to have the stone rolled away, convinced the stench of death would be the only result. Martha had no idea of the glory that could come, as he had promised, only after the initial vision for life had been snuffed out. Yet through the episode, the sisters had learned the rhythms of God that the church would soon discover as well. There would always be the birth of a vision or dream, but it would generally be followed by death of the vision and disappointment. There would be a time of burial when the dream or vision seemed impossible and the sisters would experience "the dark night of the soul." It was at this moment that *hope* had to conquer *despair* and trusting faith had to be placed in the faithfulness of God. Then, at just the right time, joy through resurrection would come in the morning. Jesus thought back to how Abraham, Sarah, Joseph, Moses,

Hannah, David, and so many of the prophets had seen initial dreams and visions dashed and buried—only to see them supernaturally fulfilled. He hoped the church would see that only after the death of their personal vision could God raise up his supernatural vision to follow.[157] The grain of wheat must fall to the ground and die if it will reap an abundant harvest.

Even from the cross Jesus began to smile as he thought about the great celebration of new life the sisters had led when Lazarus exited from the tomb. Mary was typically excited; and her emotions again got the best of her. But Martha was a sight to behold! Never had such emotion burst forth unreservedly from her. Lazarus and Mary were taken aback by the display, but new birth for her dear brother broke open her tough shell, revealing the soft center inside. Jesus recalled watching with a giant grin as the sisters administered the removal of the old clothes and the putting on of the new ones—a task Jesus would later leave to his church. Lazarus had exited the tomb all bound up. He was not walking around in freedom but was still entangled with his bandages. So, what did the sisters (and later his church) do? Jesus had told the disciples, "Whatever you loose on earth shall be loosed in heaven,"[158] and so the sisters went as the church to "unbind him and let him go."[159]

Jesus couldn't stop reminiscing about the sisters without remembering the great banquet they held in Jesus' honor. The whole village was there with Jesus as the guest of honor and Lazarus at his side. Martha had worked to make sure everything was just right, and the food was fit for a king. Jesus remembered the joy of the moment as he took bread and blessed it with the wondrously significant words, "Blessed art thou O Lord who brings forth this bread from the ground." Winking at his friend back from the ground, he broke the bread and gave it to all gathered at the table. Toasts of wine and the celebration of resurrection and Lazarus's personal comments on living the blessed life followed. Lazarus's life after life after death dominated the conversation. Everyone wanted to know what the significance of death and new life was for Lazarus—and how it could help them live a life of great value before they tasted physical death as well. Jesus looked forward to all the meals his church would spend together in celebrating his resurrection—and to the final day he would be present to preside again at the banquet table.

Jesus remembered how a lull hit the conversation at Martha's party and he looked up to see sweet Mary slipping back into the room. She was carrying something Jesus had never seen in their home before. It was beautiful—an alabaster jar she had kept hidden until just that instant. It was her savings; in it she trusted for her security. But now she wanted to use it in a beautiful and extravagant way—pouring it on Jesus' feet and wiping with her hair. The whole episode made Judas angry; it probably concerned Martha a bit too. The encounter gave everyone a surprise jolt, having never seen Mary with her hair down like that. While others formulated a theological response, Jesus received it all with gratitude and profound appreciation. He breathed deeply of the fragrant aroma and savored the moment when extravagant love was shown. He smiled at Mary and thanked her for her gift, a gift to be told about for generations to come. Mary's gift was the beautiful gift that kept on giving.

Every beautiful gift the church has given to honor Jesus through the centuries finds its roots in dear sweet Mary and her servant-hearted sister Martha as well.

FOR ALL THE SAINTS

O blest communion, fellowship divine!
We feebly struggle, they in glory shine;
Yet all are one in Thee, for all are Thine.
Alleluia, Alleluia!
And when the strife is fierce, the warfare long,
Steals on the ear the distant triumph song,
And hearts are brave, again, and arms are strong.
Alleluia, Alleluia!
The golden evening brightens in the west;
Soon, soon to faithful warriors comes their rest;
Sweet is the calm of paradise the blessed.
Alleluia, Alleluia!
But lo! there breaks a yet more glorious day;
The saints triumphant rise in bright array;
The King of glory passes on His way.
Alleluia, Alleluia!
From earth's wide bounds, from ocean's farthest coast,
Through gates of pearl streams in the countless host,
Singing to Father, Son and Holy Ghost:
Alleluia, Alleluia!

—William Walsham How, stanzas 7–11 (1823–1897)[160]

"The Next Fifty Days . . ."

Very truly I tell you, the Son can do nothing by himself; he can do only what he sees his Father doing, because whatever the Father does the Son also does. For the Father loves the Son and shows him all he does. Yes, and he will show him even greater works than these, so that you will be amazed. For just as the Father raises the dead and gives them life, even so the Son gives life to whom he is pleased to give it.

—JOHN 5:19–21

When he had received the drink, Jesus said, "It is finished." With that, he bowed his head and gave up his spirit.

—JOHN 19:30

JESUS ANNOUNCED FROM THE cross, "It is finished!" Then looking into the heavens, he closed his life, praying, "Into your hands I commit my Spirit."

At the same time, the earth shook and the rocks began to split. Tombs broke open and the bodies of many holy people who had died were raised to life as Lazarus had been. A centurion soldier who experienced the earthquake and saw the manner in which Jesus died announced, "Surely this man was the Son of God!" As Jesus gave up his Spirit, the curtain separating the holy of holies from the rest of the temple was torn asunder from top to bottom. God was thus announcing that the barrier of sin separating God and humankind had been removed—the way was now clear through Jesus for his followers to commune again with God. The viral contagion of sin and death had been fully absorbed. Jesus was now providing in himself the cure. Those who wished to live an abundant life would be injected with the life of Jesus as a vaccine able to withstand any strand of sin's viral contagion.

Those who had been complicit in Jesus' death saw and experienced the same events, but with a different result. They beat their chests and walked away smugly, feeling good about the execution just completed. Yet near the cross were many faithful women who had watched the passion unfold from a distance; among them were Mary Magdalene, Salome, Mary the mother of James, Mrs. Zebedee, and many other women who had come up to Jerusalem.[161] It appears his apostles of the past three years had scattered at the first sign of trouble—they were unwilling at that moment to accompany Jesus into death. They missed the entire crucifixion while in hiding out of fear of the Jews.

The lone apostle known to be present was John, who testified that he saw water and blood separately flowing from the pierced side of Jesus. The Jewish leaders had requested that the body of Jesus not hang on the cross over a Sabbath, and so soldiers came initially to break Jesus' legs so he would suffocate on the cross and die more quickly. Yet finding him already dead, all a soldier did was thrust his spear up into the chest cavity of Jesus, piercing his heart and figuratively the heart of his mother standing nearby as well.

A prominent member of the Sanhedrin named Joseph of Arimathea, along with his friend Nicodemus, approached the Roman governor Pilate and asked to bury the body of Jesus. Joseph had a brand new tomb, just dug for his family, and he willingly supplied it to house Jesus instead. Nicodemus came with strips of cloth and over seventy pounds of a mixture of myrrh and aloes—the same substance used at Lazarus's burial just weeks earlier. The two men wrapped the body in strips of cloth, as was the burial custom, and then placed the body on a ledge inside the tomb. Then they piled the spices upon the body, rolled a stone across the entrance, and hurried home to observe Sabbath.

There was no funeral for Jesus. Circumstances did not allow for one. Jesus died in isolation and was interred without a funeral. No one eulogized him, not even a small private ceremony occurred.

At this moment all who loved Jesus and thought he was the Lord's Messiah quarantined themselves in spiritual isolation to mourn alone, grieve alone, and wail alone. This Saturday was the darkest night of any dark night of the soul. Seemingly, all hope was gone—it had been snuffed out. The pandemic of sin had apparently taken another life, and the Devil as the grim reaper apparently had amassed another victim. If one could hear the prayers as God the Father could, all around Jerusalem and the surrounding countryside the words of David were being appropriated again: "My God, my God, why have you forsaken us?" This was the ultimate cry of abandonment: God the Father had let his Son, their Messiah, die.

Early on Sunday morning, while it was still dark, there was another violent earthquake. An angel of the Lord came down to the tomb from heaven, rolled back the stone, and sat upon it. The appearance of the angel was like lightning, and the soldiers stationed to guard the stone-sealed tomb fell down as though dead men. Not long after, just after sunrise, Mary Magdalene and some of the other women came to the tomb. They saw the stone that they wouldn't have been able to move alone already rolled back. But when they entered, they did not find the body of the Lord Jesus. As they were wondering what had happened, two angels gleaming like lightning stood beside them. One of them spoke: "Why do you look for the living among the dead? Don't be alarmed. You are looking for Jesus the Nazarene, who was crucified. He is not here; he has risen just as he said!"

The women were told to hurry and tell the disciples, especially Peter, that Jesus had indeed risen from the dead. While trembling and bewildered, the women left filled with joy and ran to go tell the disciples. When Peter and the others heard the news, both John and Peter sprinted out the door headed for the tomb. John, the younger man, won the sprint and arrived at the tomb before Peter, but did not go inside. When Peter arrived, he ran right past John and into the burial chamber, where he saw the strips of linen lying, as well as the burial cloth that had been around Jesus' head. The cloth was folded up nicely by itself, and there was an order to the strips of linen as well. Peter wondered what had happened. Finally, John joined Peter inside; and as soon as he saw the situation, he believed. This was no grave robbery; this had the look of an up-rising instead.

Mary Magdalene returned to the tomb again, just as Peter and John were leaving. This time, when she looked inside the tomb the two angels were back. They were sitting at the head and foot where Jesus' corpse had once been placed. An angel then asked her, "Woman, why are you crying?" She replied that someone had stolen the body of Jesus and she wanted to know where they had placed it. Just then, a man appeared whom Mary thought to be the gardener and asked, "Who is it you are looking for?" Then Jesus, hidden from her initial recognition, said to her, "Mary." And Mary turned and realized it was Jesus and cried out in Aramaic, "*Rabboni!*" (which means teacher). Jesus told Mary not to hold onto him but instead go present a message to the disciples. He wanted them to continue in isolation a bit longer, and he would soon appear to them.

On Sunday afternoon Jesus appeared incognito along the road to Emmaus with two of his disciples. He was again hidden from being recognized, and explained to the two travelers how Jesus' death and resurrection was the plan and the prophecy of the Old Testament Scriptures. As he explained text after text, the men's hearts burned with a passion as they grasped the unfolding divine plan being carried to completion in their day. Arriving at their destination, the two travelers invited Jesus to join them for supper. Jesus hesitated, but did so. At dinner, Jesus was handed the bread to say the blessing. As he spoke the words, "Blessed art thou O Lord, who brings forth this bread from the ground," Jesus' real presence was revealed to the two men in the breaking of the bread. Then Jesus vanished from their midst. The two men immediately rose up, got dressed again, and traveled back to Jerusalem to share what they had seen and learned.

Meanwhile, back in Jerusalem, the apostles had locked themselves in the upper room, fearing the Jews (there was a rumor being falsely spread that they had stolen the body). Yet Jesus soon appeared in their midst and greeted them, "Shalom be upon you all." He asked them for some food to feed his resurrected body and ate the broiled fish in their presence—Jesus was no ghost. He then breathed upon his followers and said, "Receive the Holy Spirit." Thomas was missing from the gathering that evening, and the others told him of Jesus' miraculous entrance. They had played tricks on him before, so he doubted: "Unless I see the nail marks and put my finger where the nails were, I will not believe it." A week later, the apostles were gathered again in the same place when Jesus appeared. Jesus invited Thomas to touch him and stop doubting, but at that point Thomas cried out, "My Lord and my God."

During the following period of forty days, Jesus appeared again and again . . . to Peter over a charcoal fire (where he invited the one who denied him three times to profess his devotion on three occasions), to the Twelve (both in Jerusalem and at Galilee), to over five hundred believers who gathered all at the same time (surely Martha, Mary, and Lazarus were part of this mass gathering!), and then to his brother James (who once found Jesus crazy but later became the pillar of the Jerusalem church). One can imagine he spoke with his mother, Mary, and with the women who traveled along with him, but no records of those visits are certain. Jesus did many other miraculous signs not written down by his disciples, but those recorded lead one to the life that is really living.

On one occasion, while Jesus was eating with the apostles, he gave them this command:

> Do not leave Jerusalem, but wait for the gift my Father promised, which you have heard me speak about. For John baptized with water, but in a few days you will be baptized with the Holy Spirit. (Acts 1:4–5)

At that meeting the apostles asked Jesus, "Lord, are you now going to restore the kingdom of Israel to her former glory?" Jesus then replied,

> It is not for you to know the times or dates the Father has set by his own authority. But you will receive power when the Holy Spirit comes on you; and you will be my witnesses in Jerusalem, and in all Judea and Samaria, and to the ends of the earth. (Acts 1:7–8)

After these words, Jesus ascended into the heavens—taken up in bodily form before their very eyes.

The apostles returned to Jerusalem and gathered regularly to pray for the outpouring of the Holy Spirit. Jesus had promised this Spirit as a guardian, guide, and schoolmaster who would guide them into all things. This Spirit that had created a world without the contagion of sin would now redeem all that was infected and turned to Jesus for healing. Jesus had insisted life with and in the Spirit would be better for them than while he was physically present. Whatever that meant, the faithful prayed fervently for such a gift! There were around 120 who gathered regularly in the upper room, including Jesus' mother, Mary—and all of Jesus' once-doubting brothers. For the next ten days, through prayer, fasting, and the *peshers*[162] found in the Psalms, the apostles sought the pouring out of the Holy Spirit that Jesus had promised.

Finally, on Pentecost (the Jewish feast celebrating the spring harvest) there was a sound like the blowing of a violent wind crashing against the house where they gathered. Then they saw what looked like tongues of fire coming to rest upon each of them. The apostles began to speak, and the Spirit enabled them to communicate in languages previously unknown to them. This occurred because Pentecost had drawn dispersed Jews from around the world to come to Jerusalem for the feast. Jews from every tongue and nationality were amazed to hear the wonders of God described to them in their mother tongue. Amazed that untrained Galileans had such linguistic gifts, folks began to ask, "What does it all mean?"

With that, Peter stood on the southern steps of the temple and announced to all the unfolding plan of God in Jesus the Messiah. Peter explained how the prophet Joel had prophesied about the day's unfolding events and that the great King David had foretold Jesus' coming resurrection almost a thousand years earlier. Jesus of Nazareth, put to death on a cross by wicked men, had been raised from the dead by God. Jesus was free from the agony of death; death had no hold on him. Peter explained,

> God has raised this Jesus to life, and we are all witnesses of it. Exalted to the right hand of God, he has received from the Father the promised Holy Spirit and has poured out what you now see and hear. (Acts 2:32–33)

The Spirit poured out was the gift Jesus received from the Father—he now breathed it out upon his church. Peter continued, "Therefore let all Israel be assured of this: God has made this Jesus, whom you crucified, both Lord and Messiah."

These words cut to the heart of the people gathered, and many began to cry out, "What can we do about what we have done?" Peter replied, "Repent," turn from your past misdeeds and turn toward God. He continued, "And be baptized, every one of you, in the name of Jesus Christ for the forgiveness of your sins." All around Peter stood hundreds of *miqvahs* (Jewish purification baptistries) where Peter now entreated each person to save themselves from this corrupt generation. Those baptized experienced the forgiveness of sin and received the Holy Spirit Jesus had promised to his followers before he ascended.

Those who accepted Peter's message that day were baptized, and God did for them all that Jesus had promised: they were healed of their sin, vaccinated spiritually with the life of Jesus within, and they received a gift of the Holy Spirit. About three thousand were added to their number on that one day; among them must have been the three disciples from nearby Bethany: Mary, Martha, and Lazarus.

HYMN 1

My intellect sees what has happened,
But it cannot explain it;
It can see, and wishes to explain,
But can find no word that suffices,
For what it sees is invisible and entirely formless,

Simple, completely uncompounded,
Unbounded in its awesome greatness.
What I have seen is the totality recapitulated as One,
Received not in essence but by participation.
It is just as if you lit a flame from a live flame:
It is the entire flame you receive.

—Saint Symeon the New Theologian (949–1022)[163]

Chapter Thirteen (Conclusion)

You've Now Been Cast as "Lazarus"

Having once gotten through death, to come back and then, at some later date, have all her dying to do over again? They call Stephen the first martyr. Hadn't Lazarus the rawer deal?

—C. S. Lewis

To be commanded to love God at all, let alone in the wilderness, is like being commanded to be well when we are sick, to sing for joy when we are dying of thirst, to run when our legs are broken. But this is the first and greatest commandment nonetheless. Even in the wilderness—especially in the wilderness—you shall love him.

—Frederick Buechner

Early church traditions have proposed various accounts of the rest of the life of Lazarus. Some have him going to Cyprus and dying there in AD 63. Other have him living and dying again in his own home town of Bethany. This is an imaginative attempt based on Scripture to describe how he lived out his days and the type of impact he made in and around Bethany.

Lazarus stood in a long line, just off the southern steps outside the temple. He was waiting his turn in a throng of men chanting the psalms of Pentecost, as they waited to be baptized in Jesus' name. The sisters were not with him, they were off in another area where crowds of women waited in even longer lines. There was much singing and dancing as person after person would step up to the baptismal *miqvah*, disrobe, and make their way down seven small steps into the deepest part of the ceremonial pool. There one of the 120 who had been praying for the coming of the Spirit would ask each person two significant questions: 1) "Do you believe that Jesus of Nazareth is the Lord's Messiah, the rightful ruler of all things?" and 2) "What is your good confession about Jesus?" The answers to the two questions among those coming to be baptized varied a bit, one from another. However, that day over three thousand came stating that Jesus had ascended to God's right hand and taken his rightful place as the King of the Universe and as Lord of their lives. Caesar may sit enthroned in Rome and rule an empire, but their Lord was greater than Caesar. King Jesus sits enthroned above the cosmos and has dominion over all things!

As Lazarus waited patiently, memories from Bethany weeks earlier gave fresh meaning to his current state. Since emerging from the family tomb, he simply could not view the world the same way again. It was still a beautiful and grand creation, but he could sense its groaning under the onslaught of decay—it longed to be renewed. And Lazarus had felt in his own body this same longing. Lazarus had been raised from the dead, but he had not been given a new and glorious resurrected body.[164] He was still a middle-aged man, had a bit of a belly on him, and was losing his eyesight as well as his hair. He might still outwork the younger men when he had to, but getting out of bed the following morning was a chore in itself. He had not yet received an immortal body and could get sick again—perhaps from the same strain of virus. A resurrected body like Jesus now had since those forty days of appearances was not his yet. Lazarus was longing for what Paul later described:

> We know that the whole creation has been groaning as in the pains of childbirth right up to the present time. Not only so, but we our- selves, who have the first fruits of the Spirit, groan inwardly as we wait eagerly for our adoption to sonship, the redemption of our bodies. (Rom 8:22–23)

Lazarus wanted more than to be brought back to life; he longed for the redemption of his body.

Lazarus had died of the virus and was subject to decay because of sin. Lazarus had descended into Hades and had seen the consequences of life's choices firsthand. Hades was a big place, hosting the faithful until final redemption in an amazing heavenly paradise—a mansion with gardens and heavenly hosts. There some slept, others lounged and rested, speaking with saints from other eras. They were all awaiting the trumpet blast and the final redemption when the New Jerusalem would come down and they would rule on earth over cities, villages, and hamlets for King Jesus.

But for others, there was a great chasm separating the realm of the unrighteous from the righteous—they were thrown into a dung heap called Gehenna. It was a place of worms and decay, where Satan ruled as "the Lord of the Flies." Lazarus could see the agony, and hear the weeping and gnashing of teeth. People sentenced there called to him for even a cup of water—but he could do nothing to help them. It was more gruesome than he imagined, and he heard the regret of a life wasted in the moaning cries of those suffering in torment there. Sin was ugly; it was horrible; it was deadly. Sin was real and had real consequences. It was the true viral contagion. How each person lived on earth would have eternal consequences and massive implications.

Lazarus had returned from the dead knowing another truth too. He, Lazarus, the one Jesus called "beloved," was a slave to sin as well. As much as he loved Jesus, he had at times chosen the wide road that led to death. Lazarus committed sins and was himself a sinner. The sin that had subjected the world to decay had bitten him too. That ancient serpent, the Devil, had been hurled down to earth after losing the cosmic battle of heaven[165] and was making war against God's people for a short time—until his final defeat and destruction. Lazarus was snake-bitten by sin, infected with its virus. The Devil had gotten the best of him, and thus the venom of death had entered his body and had begun to kill him. Not only was the death of sin killing him, it was injuring his relationships with others as well. Lazarus saw the effects of this greatest viral pandemic in the lives of his friends, his neighbors, and his community—even in his sisters. Lazarus may have been Jesus' best friend, may have been raised from the dead, and may have had notoriety because of it. But Lazarus still had a sin problem, and Jesus held the only antidote. Jesus was the vaccine that would heal him for good, forever. Lazarus was famous because Jesus had raised him once, but he still needed "the famous one" to do something about the emptiness sin had placed inside him that fame could do nothing to erase.

Finally, Lazarus stepped into the top step of the baptistry. He disrobed quietly as an act of bodily prayer, offering all of himself naked and needy to a gracious Father to forgive. Generations earlier, Adam and Eve had tried to sew fig leaves to cover the shame of their sin from God; however, Lazarus acknowledged his and came vulnerably naked before the Lord. As he stepped down each of the seven stairs deeper into the pool, he mouthed the words "Jesus is Lord" over and over again. Standing in the deep part of the pool, a disciple asked him two questions. Boldly and confidently Lazarus replied, "I believe and know that Jesus is Lord and Messiah, my best friend, and the redeemer of my life." Lazarus had died before, and Jesus had raised him—but still as Lazarus. Now he was dying to the old Lazarus, the sin-filled Lazarus with the virus of death within him. He would soon arise as a new creation with Jesus as the hope of glory within him.

As he stood at the deep end of the *miqvah,* the disciple sitting on the ledge of the baptistry placed his hand upon the head of Lazarus. "I now baptize you," he said, "in the name of the Father, the Son, and the Holy Spirit for the forgiveness of your sins and that you might receive the promised Holy Spirit." Before the disciple could plunge Lazarus down into the pool, Lazarus spoke. "Hold me down there a while, please," Lazarus requested, "I've got a lot to think about." And with that, Lazarus began to take a large breath, but before he was fully ready, the disciple plunged his head down into the pool.

As Lazarus entered baptism's watery grave, he began to think back over the last two months. His death. His burial. His resurrection at Jesus' command. Then there was Jesus' death. Jesus' burial. And then Jesus' resurrection at the Father's command. He knew this moment beneath the waters gave new meaning and fresh context to all the matters of life and death he had gone through before. He was experiencing again, for a brief moment, that spiritual isolation in time between death and resurrection—between old life and new creation.

Still holding his breath beneath the watery grave, Lazarus began to pray: "Lord Jesus, may your death, burial, and resurrection give meaning to my new life. Through my baptism, I die to sin and to my sinful nature, and I join you in your death. You raised me once from the dead to show your power over death; now raise me again through the glory of your Father that I might gain a resurrected body and new life in you. I want to rise with you Jesus, and I want to live through you where sin and death have no mastery over me."[166] Lazarus paused to consider what should be his first words upon rising from the waters of baptism to his new reality. He knew. Pushing up with his legs from the bottom of the baptismal pool his body shot up out of the water. Throwing his head back and flinging water through the air he shouted, "Hallelujah! New creation!"

Lazarus walked up a second set of stairs to exit the pool, knowing that the sinful powers of the Evil One had been disarmed. He left his sinful nature behind—it had been put off. There was a freedom and an inner purity he had not felt when he was raised in Bethany. This time, Jesus had done more than raise him from the dead; he had washed him and made him new. As he walked up the seven stairs to exit, his robe was handed back to him again. Slipping it on, a disciple whispered to him, "If you have been baptized into Jesus the Messiah, you have been clothed with him. No matter your race, legal status, or gender you are part of the oneness in Christ—you have become Abraham's true seed and an heir of what God promised him so long ago."[167] Lazarus, full of joy and new life, smiled—then went looking for his sisters to celebrate together.

Lazarus had agreed to meet the sisters up on the platform leading to the southern steps—near the statue to the prophetess Huldah. From there was easy access to the temple through Solomon's Portico. Standing on the platform, where Peter had preached just a few hours earlier, he could see people from every tribe and tongue (people speaking Arabic,[168] Egyptian, Greek, and Hebrew as well as other languages he couldn't even recognize) pledging their lives to Jesus as King. People were being baptized in every *miqvah*, and some were lining up almost a mile away at the Pool of Siloam. *Today is Pentecost*, Lazarus thought, *and the Lord of the Harvest is gathering in his children from all across the world. This is so much more than I could have ever asked or imagined!* He saw his sisters coming up the stairs to meet him—more joyous than he had ever seen them!

Martha and Mary spoke of a new realization in this moment: "Only things that die can be resurrected," they said. They realized baptism had been a spiritual death and a resurrection for them now as well. In a spiritual sense, they were now living into life after death while looking forward to the life after life after death still to come. The family never imagined there could be a day that would top the raising of Lazarus, but Jesus had provided one in less than two months. THIS was the best day of their lives—no doubt!

In the midst of the celebration was a realization that God had done something new, but what did it all mean? The apostles were gathered in prayer and discussion in Solomon's Portico trying to sort out what should follow. Having heard from their Lord Jesus through the inner guidance of the Spirit, they came down to tell the crowd of new Jesus-followers what should ensue. Peter began to talk, and sometimes when he talked, he talked too much. But the basic message to the crowd of excited followers was, "Since you have been raised with the Messiah, set your hearts on the things above, where King Jesus sits enthroned at the right hand of God in heaven. Set your minds on the things above—the things Jesus taught us while among us. Today by your baptism, you died to your old self, your life is now hidden with the Messiah in God our Father. So keep putting to death the sinful deeds of your earthly nature—that is not you anymore! Be pure, be holy, be generous, be faithful, be true to your word and honest in your speech. The Messiah is now your all in all."[169]

To help believers walk out this new identity as new creation, the apostles asked everyone to join a discipleship group. These gatherings would meet in homes where apostles could pass on the basics of the Jesus way of life (later called the *Christ*ian faith). The apostles would tell of their three-year encounter with Jesus and give new followers the tools to grow and develop as Messiah-followers as well. These groups would devote themselves to the life of disciples, with the goal of soon becoming "disciple-makers"—those who lead others to embrace the faith as well. The basic tools of devotion for followers of this Way were: the apostles' teaching, the togetherness of community, the eucharist and fellowship meals, and the praying of the Psalms at the times of prayer.[170] The apostles then began asking for people willing to host a discipleship group in their home. Lazarus looked over at Martha to see if she wanted to host, but she was already gone. One can imagine the line forming behind Martha!

Afterwards, others from Bethany who had pledged their allegiance to King Jesus through the waters of baptism traveled back together. It was a two-mile journey from the southern steps to their village on the other side of the Mount of Olives. As they reached the bottom of the Kidron Valley that would begin the summit to the crest of the Mount of Olives, Lazarus focused upon the garden of Gethsemane immediately to their right. How often had Jesus camped nearby, and how often had Lazarus found him beginning or ending a day in prayer there? Judas had known to look for him there on the betrayal night, because every evening seemed to end there before Jesus returned to the campsite and to bed. Lazarus suggested they all pause to pray in Jesus' favorite location as well.

From Gethsemane, Jesus had prayed that all his disciples might be one, just as Father and Son were one. He had prayed for a unity and a devotion to truth. And now, with one heart and voice, and with a unity of the

Spirit, this small band of new converts began to pray as Jesus had taught them.

> Our Father in heaven, hallowed be your name. Your Kingdom come; your will be done on earth as it is in heaven. Give us this day the bread we need for today, and forgive us in the manner we forgive others. Lead us away from temptation and deliver us from evil. The kingdom, power, and glory are yours forever and ever. Amen.

Lazarus closed the prayer by reminding them all of the power of the Holy Spirit now residing within each of them: "May that Spirit pour the love of Jesus into your hearts that you might know how long, and high, and wide, and deep is the love of Jesus our Lord. Good night." And with that, the group headed towards their homes for some rest at the end of a most amazing day.

In the days which followed, Lazarus, his sisters, and the other believers in Bethany found themselves drawn to the synagogue. Like Jesus himself, they were still Jewish, and the synagogue was still their gathering place. In Jesus himself, they saw the fulfillment of their Jewish faith and not a break from it. Jesus was the fulfillment of every prophecy and the hope of every prophet. Each time they gathered in the synagogue and began to read from the law, the prophets, or the Psalms someone would speak up, saying, "That passage was speaking about Jesus!" With great excitement, they read Scripture with fresh eyes to see Jesus on every page. They prayed more fervently than ever before, knowing the Spirit joined them in their praying. They fasted regularly for a lost world[171] and for the needs of their city. As the "awakened ones," they now prayed Jesus would, by the power of the Holy Spirit, "Awaken Bethany/Awaken Jerusalem."[172] They walked the streets of Bethany looking for God's prodigal sons and daughters ready to return to their loving Father. The names "Jesus" and "Christ/Messiah" were such a part of their vocabulary that people began to call them the "Christians"— those that talk about Jesus the Messiah all the time. They shared their food, their clothing, and their money, but never their bedrooms or their spouses. They were generous people. But they were also pure and holy people.

Lazarus went back to work, but he was a noticeably different boss. He wanted to be a "spiritual leader" and to model the kind of servant leadership Jesus had shown his disciples. He hired a retired rabbi to work for him as a "corporate chaplain."[173] This highly respected man checked on each worker's well-being, family life, and pressing concerns. These pressing concerns became the subject and substance of many of Lazarus's prayers as he now tried to absorb the grief of his employees. He began to love his workers and care deeply about their families. He began to thank God for the business he was stewarding which allowed him to bless families and shape future generations. His workers soon began to take a greater pride in the business as well. Soon they were consumed with quality, value, and craftsmanship. Workers showed him ways to improve the products he offered and even encouraged him to stay true to a value proposition that made them a Bethany favorite. In the coming years Lazarus's business made the *Jerusalem Post* as one of the "Best Places to Work" and a "Leading Innovation" company.

But what really excited Lazarus about his business was the opportunity to give back to the Bethany community. Remember, the name "Lazarus" means "God helps." And the city Lazarus resided within was called "Bethany"—the "house of affliction." Bethany was where the unclean and the broken resided when they were no longer welcome in Jerusalem near the temple. Bethany was a city for the marginalized and the broken. But Lazarus decided to change the narrative about Bethany. He loved Bethany, not because it was already loveable, but because it was his home. One day in the synagogue, the scroll of Jeremiah was read, and the words pierced Lazarus's heart and gave new purpose to his days on the earth:

> Also, seek the peace and prosperity of the city to which I have carried you into exile. Pray to the Lord for it, because if it prospers, you too will prosper. (Jer 29:7)

From that point forward, Lazarus decided to use his time after his physical resurrection (his raising) and spiritual rebirth (his baptism) to live into his name and alter the perception of his hometown. He looked around everywhere and thought, *We can't have things looking like this when King Jesus returns! People need food and shelter, and no one should live on the street. The community parks need benches and trees, and the creek needs to be cleaned. The neighbor's house needs paint, and the widow's roof is in need of repairs. It just won't do for things to be like this when Jesus comes back!* Lazarus had no intention of being embarrassed by the living conditions in his community when the Lord returned. He was going to have to give an account of how he spent his five talents.

Lazarus started asking, "What if, with God's help, we could bring rebirth and renewal to this whole city—doing what Jesus wants done here? What would that look like?" He took a long weekend and asked himself, "What if I gave my time, my talent, and my treasure to bring good news to the poor and recovery of sight to the blind, to lift up the oppressed, and to usher in the time of God's favor?[174] How would God's Spirit help bring this about through me?" In so doing, Lazarus began living into his name, "God helps," and did much to change the city. Soon people began wondering: Could Bethany even be called a "house of affliction" anymore? The city was being transformed and renewed, Jesus' kingdom had come, and his will was being done in that little space on earth—just as it was in heaven.

As news of this transformation led by the one known as "Jesus' best friend" made the rounds in Jerusalem, the religious leaders decided to kill Lazarus. His life was a great a witness[175] for Jesus; he needed to be executed:

> So the chief priests made plans to kill Lazarus as well, for on account of him many of the Jews were going over to Jesus and putting their faith in him. (John 12:10–11)

When people came to warn Lazarus of the bounty on his head, Lazarus did not shrink back from what he was doing—not one bit. He was ready to give up what he could not keep to gain what could never be lost. His sisters counseled *safety* for their brother Lazarus, but they knew what he cared most deeply about was *significance*—he wanted his life to matter. He no longer feared those who could kill the body, for he knew a resurrected and glorious body that would never fade away was just ahead—so close he could almost touch it. He wanted all things renewed, and he wasn't satisfied to play it safe when eternity was at stake.

No one knows exactly how Lazarus finally died. Was he martyred or did he die again from another virus—or even from old age? But one day before he died, his sisters asked him what final thing he wanted done in his honor when he departed. He answered with a smile on his face, "Plant a tree."[176]

When the news of Lazarus's falling asleep reached the township, there was a profound sadness at his death but a great celebration of the one who had lived so well among them. Lazarus used his "second chance at life" to live life to the fullest—no regrets. Not only was Lazarus a changed man because of Jesus, but Bethany was a changed city through him as well. The entire region mourned his loss. The city leaders gathered at the gate to discuss what should be done to remember the one who did so much for them all. "Bethany" as the "house of affliction" was a name no longer fit for the town. The town had a different spirit now. The city leaders decided it was time. It was time to change the city's name going forward.

One of the city fathers spoke up with this suggestion, "Why not 'El 'Azariiyeh,' the 'City of Lazarus'?" They were, after all, the city "God Helped" because Lazarus had helped make beauty out of ashes. They all agreed. It was evident to all that the one Jesus raised from the dead had then raised his hometown to a new life as well.

And the city is still called "El 'Azariiyeh"—"The City of Lazarus"— even to this day.

EXPOSTULATION XXI

My God, my God, how large a glass of the next world is this!
As we have an art, to cast from one glass to another,
and so to carry the species a great way off,
so hast thou, that way, much more;
we shall have a resurrection in heaven;
the knowledge of that thou castest by another glass upon us here;
we feel that we have a resurrection from sin,
and that by another glass too;
we see we have a resurrection of the body
from the miseries and calamities of this life.

This resurrection of my body shows
me the resurrection of my soul;
and both here severally, of both together hereafter.
Since thy martyrs under the altar press thee with their solicitation
for the resurrection of the body to glory, thou wouldst pardon me,
if I should press thee by prayer
for the accomplishing of this resurrection,
which thou hast begun in me, to health.

But, O my God, I do not ask, where I might ask amiss,
nor beg that which perchance might be worse for me.
I have a bed of sin; delight in sin is a bed:
I have a grave of sin; senselessness of sin is a grave:
and where Lazarus had been four days,
I have been fifty years in this putrefaction;
why dost thou not call me, as thou didst him, with a loud voice,
since my soul is as dead as his body was?
I need thy thunder, O my God; thy music will not serve me.

—John Donne (1572–1631)[177]

Jesus in Isolation (Implications)
Lazarus, Viruses, and Us

I do not ask the wounded person how he feels, I myself become the wounded person.

—WALT WHITMAN

Die before you die. There is no chance after.

—C. S. LEWIS

1. *Your personal story is really a story about Jesus—and his life revealed in you.*

   The entire miracle of the raising of Lazarus is told in only two verses. Almost the whole narrative tells the *real* story, which is about Jesus at work. The same is true for you. Whatever you are going through today, let it be Jesus' story revealed in you. God is revealing the glorious riches of this mystery: "Christ in you, the hope of glory" (Col 1:27).

2. *God's ways will not always make sense to us. If they did, he would not be God.*

   The case against God can be easily stated from the Lazarus story this way: *How can two sisters trust and love a God who let their brother die?* If God is both loving and powerful, why did Lazarus die before his time? This is the greatest challenge to the Christian faith among those who are agnostic or atheists. God's countersuit against the sisters can likewise be stated: *If God's children do not suffer, they are not wise. If they are not wise, they are not blessed. Therefore, if they do not suffer, how can they be blessed?*[178]

3. *It is okay to question God, and even cry out in frustration towards him.*
King David was known as "the man after God's own heart," and he modeled for those who follow after him how to respond to Almighty God. Read the Psalms, beginning with Psalm 22, to see the amazing "conversation of the heart" David shared with God. David's cry of abandonment, "My God, my God, why have you forsaken me?" was given as a gift to God-followers who would come after David, that we might have a rich language from which to speak to a Holy God.

4. *No matter how deep our darkness, God is still deeper.*
When Mary and Martha were at their darkest moment, Jesus showed that the words of the psalmist were true: "Even the darkness will not be dark to you" (Ps 139:12), for in Jesus is light that shines out of darkness. As it was for David it will be for you: "The Lord turned my darkness into light" (2 Sam 22:29).

5. *Being Jesus' friend is a worthy life pursuit. Make it your own.*
Followers of Jesus can transition from living as a *servant* of Jesus to being a *friend*. John tells us so in John 15:15: "I no longer call you servants, because a servant does not know his master's business. Instead, I have called you friends, for everything that I learned from my Father I have made known to you." You can develop a friendship with Jesus by treating him as an ever-present friend.

6. *Whatever challenges come your way, send them to Jesus in prayer.*
Mary and Martha knew to send their concerns on to Jesus. The distinguishing feature of the early church was a commitment to prayer and fasting. The church gathered in the waiting room of the upper room to pray and wait for the Spirit (Acts 1:14); they continued in prayer after Pentecost (Acts 2:42), and prayer with fasting empowered their mission (Acts 13:2–3). Perhaps Archbishop William Temple said it best: "When I pray, coincidences happen, when I don't, they don't."[179]

7. *When crises come, and things are beyond what you can bear, place them into the hands of Jesus. He will absorb your grief.*
S. D. Gordon once said, "You can do more than pray *after* you have prayed, but you cannot do more than pray until you have prayed."[180]

God neither sleeps, slumbers, nor walks away—He is always present and ready to listen to our prayers. Mary and Martha found peace when *their* concern became *Jesus'* concern too. Through prayer we learn not to be anxious about anything, but in everything to take it to Jesus in prayer. There we exchange our anxiety for a peace from God that passes all understanding (see Phil 4:6–7).

8. *Spiritual isolation is where God places us to grow through what we go through.*

    Not every lesson can be learned in quick-time; some things require waiting, isolation, and trusting in the Lord. This was true for Jesus, Martha and Mary, and even Lazarus. Phillip Yancy says it succinctly: "Pain turned you to God."[181] The earliest Christians learned to wait with eager expectation for Jesus' presence to come and save. Jesus always arrives on time, but never early.

9. *In the isolation and spiritual distancing, we must embrace "productive suffering."*

    Lazarus was called to embrace "productive suffering," and so are we. Athletes and pregnant women both labor and strive through suffering in order to produce a glorious result. C. S. Lewis once said, "You never know how much you really believe anything until its truth or falsehood becomes a matter of life and death to you."[182]

10. *In the isolation God reveals what you really believe—trust him.*

    The waiting is worth the pain, as nothing worth having comes without effort.

11. *While in social distancing and isolation, use the time there to serve others.*

    There are three types of people in the world: a) *energy-drainers* suck the life out of every situation and bring others down, b) *energy-neutral* people neither make a situation better or worse, they are there solely for themselves and never notice another, and c) *energy-givers* make things better for everyone else and bring life and vitality to a room. Be an energy-giver in the isolation and distancing; make it better in the ways you can for someone else. Jesus kept serving others, even as his heart was focused upon Lazarus in Bethany.

12. *God will not answer us on our timetable, but only on his own. Learn patience and obedience through the suffering.*

   Jesus had to wait in isolation for two days before responding to Mary and Martha's message—that was God the Father's timing. There is only one sovereign Lord of the Universe, and it is not you. Let God be God—and trust in his timing that he has your best interests at heart. He honest-to-God does; it's true.

13. *For the Jesus follower, death is as falling asleep.*

   Death does not end the relationship a believer has with God, it simply means a "falling asleep." We fall asleep only when we feel safe, secure, and protected—and confident we will arise happily again. For the Christian, sleep is that state we enter when we trust God enough to enter into his rest.

14. *Those who sleep in death with the Lord will wake up.*

   Those who sleep in death do wake up. When Jesus told his disciples, "Lazarus is asleep" and he was going to wake him up, the disciples keenly replied, "If he sleeps, he will get up." Those who sleep in the Lord *do* get up—to everlasting life. You can count on it. Paul promises this for our encouragement in 1 Thess 4:16–18.

15. *Discipleship entails carrying a cross and following Jesus into death.*

   Thomas invited the other apostles, and us in our hearing, to journey with Jesus that we might die with him. This is the call to discipleship. Jesus explained, "If anyone would come after me, he must deny himself, take up his cross and follow me" (Mark 8:34). Bonhoeffer later summarized this as, "When Christ calls a man, he bids him come and die."[183]

16. *Our presence in another's grief (absorbing his or her pain) is a present to them.*

   When you don't know what to say or do during the grief of another, be present as you can. We must show up in the ways available to us. Be present; your presence is a present that will not be undervalued or forgotten. And until another is relieved of pain, use their pain as your call to prayer.

17. *Jesus is "resurrection"—life after life after death only comes through him.*

   Those who die in the Lord have fallen asleep in Jesus. They are still alive to God, even in this moment. The resurrection to come will involve life again . . . after the present circumstance of life after death in the waiting place. Later, those who are dead will return to the new earth to reign and rule with Christ (this is life after life after death).

18. *Joy is a giant, while grief is her dwarf.*
    The Christian life is filled with immeasurable amounts of a joy that come from being a child of God and a sibling of King Jesus. Sorrow and grief last for a moment, but joy arrives again in the morning. Embrace joy—it is a giant.

19. *Jesus is "life"—the only life that is truly living is found by, through, and in him.*
    The definition of "really living" is to know Jesus—to know the power of his resurrection, share in his suffering, and become like him now in death. This is what Lazarus experiences and what Jesus promises us. Abundant life is lived by imitating Jesus.

20. *"Heaven" or "paradise" is where Lazarus went to await final resurrection. Heaven became his "waiting room" until Jesus would call him forth again.*
    "Heaven" is the abode of God. "Paradise" is his beautiful garden. Lazarus is presently in heaven as you read these words; he is enjoying paradise along with his sisters. Just as before, Lazarus is there again now awaiting a call from Jesus to return again—this time to a new earth and New Jerusalem. Next time Jesus calls him (and us), Lazarus will receive a new and glorious resurrected body—not the same one he had before.

21. *The ultimate "home" for Lazarus is not "heaven" or "paradise"—those were names for his waiting room in Hades. His final destination will come when he is again called out of the grave to join Jesus, in a new heaven and new earth.*
    The dead in Christ will rise first, and this includes Lazarus, Martha, and Mary. Those still alive (perhaps this is us!) will join them in the air and welcome Jesus to a new earth together. They will leave heaven and paradise to return to God's new earth prepared for us.

22. *Miracles do happen, often in answer to the prayers of the faithful.*
    Jesus is not limited by the laws of science or nature; he created them. That which is impossible for humankind is quite possible for God. As the angel told the Virgin Mary, "Nothing is impossible with God"

(Luke 1:37). Sisters Mary and Martha knew the presence of Jesus could change things miraculously—this is still the case. Prayer and fasting are still the best way to bring the power and presence of Jesus' Spirit to bear in the lives of those seeking a miracle.

23. *Jesus holds power over sin and death—Satan is no match for him.*
In John's Revelation we are given a vision of the resurrected Jesus, who says, "I am the First and Last. I am the Living One; I was dead, and behold I am alive for ever and ever! And I hold the keys of death and Hades" (Rev 1:17–18). Lazarus knew what sin allowed Satan to do to humankind, but also experienced the power of Jesus to conquer sin and death. Jesus holds the keys to the future and is awaiting his Father's instruction to fully inaugurate the new kingdom.

24. *Lazarus experienced death, burial, and then bodily resurrection by Jesus; yet he still needed the death, burial, and resurrection of Jesus to give his life meaning and purpose.*
Lazarus was still in sin and a person to be pitied for coming back to life again—until Jesus' own death, burial, and resurrection gave his life meaning. Lazarus's physical body would die again, but Jesus' resurrection gave him new life and hope. This promise of a resurrection body comes only after the resurrection of the Lord Jesus secures this promise for us.

25. *Lazarus was not the "awakened one" after his resurrection but trusted in Jesus as the awakened one who could awaken anyone.*
Buddha's entire philosophy centered around his answer to the problem of suffering. His answer came from descending deeply into the pain and mystery of suffering. His actual name was Gotama Siddhartha; "Buddha" was not his name but a title, like "Messiah" or "Lord." The name "Buddha" means "awakened one"—but we know of one "still awakened," as Jesus lives never to die again. Buddha shared his message of *balance* and *embracing suffering as a path* to help his followers live fuller and more meaningful lives. But those who know Jesus, as Lazarus did, know Jesus is the "truly awakened one never to die again." Jesus has a better answer for suffering and the "awakened life" than Buddha.

26. *We participate in the death, burial, and resurrection of Jesus through baptism.*

Lazarus had his own physical death, burial, and resurrection into a life after life after death. But it was his participation through baptism in the death, burial, and resurrection of Jesus that saved him and gave him the promise of an eternal life and life after death. Baptism is a "burial with Christ that we too, might be raised to new life" (see Rom 6:1–11).

27. *When Jesus returns again, we will go out to meet him in the air and usher him into the new earth and New Jerusalem coming down. Our ultimate "home" is not heaven, but a new earth.*
As Martha and Mary went out to meet Jesus on the outskirts of Bethany, so the faithful in Christ will rise up to meet Jesus in the air at his Second Coming (1 Thess 4:17). We will then escort our arriving king into his new kingdom and the New Jerusalem coming down from heaven (see Rev 21:1–5).

28. *At Jesus' return, those in Christ will receive spiritual bodies like Jesus received after his resurrection. We will not be disembodied spirits, but will have glorious immortal bodies.*
The body that dies is corruptible and earthly, but the new body that will be raised is spiritual and eternal (see 1 Cor 15:35–44). At the Second Coming of Jesus the believers will all be changed, and the mortal will put on immortality.

29. *Until Jesus returns, we as the church gathered are to: pray, embrace the word of God, commune with Jesus at the table of the Lord, live holy lives, love through fellowship, share good news, and work for gospel justice.*
The earliest disciples devoted themselves to the things of Jesus mentioned above (see Acts 2:42–48). They viewed their baptism as having raised them with Christ, and so set their minds on the things of Jesus Christ (see Col 3:1–11).

30. *Until Jesus returns, we as the church scattered are to pray and study, love our families as Jesus loves his church, disciple our friends and children into the Lord, work for God's reign and rule in our businesses, schools and communities, and look forward to Lord's imminent return.*
This is a task worthy of your greatest effort. May God bless you!

Discussion Questions

For videos by the author designed to introduce each chapter's discussion questions visit *wscottsager.com*

CHAPTER ONE:

1. What is your favorite thing to do to pass the time when you are bored? Have you ever found it a time waster? Why?

2. Where does boredom come from? How is it related to our expectations? Is it ever a response to isolation and waiting?

3. What causes spiritual boredom? Have you ever been spiritually tired like King David and just wanted to check out and have a break? How vulnerable does this make you to poor choices?

4. Read Psalm 22 as though you were sitting next to David as he composed it. What most strikes you about David's pain? What strikes you about his insights into the human condition?

5. Describe David's concern for his son Absalom before the battle. Is that normal for a father to feel towards a son? How must David have felt as he awaited news about him from the battlefront?

6. What words could be used to describe the pain David felt at the news of the death of his son? How did he feel about having no funeral for his son? How would you feel if you were one his soldiers at that moment?

7. Recite David's words "My God, my God, why have you forsaken me" out loud with the tone and emphasis you believe David would have used.

8. Have words similar to David's ever been your own words as well? What brought you to that point? Did the words help?

CHAPTER TWO:

1. Have you ever had someone you could genuinely call your best friend? What makes for a best friend in your estimation?

2. Imagine being Jesus' best friend. What might you have in common to build a friendship upon? What role would you play in his life, and he in yours? How might the distance between the two of you shape the friendship and acts of friendship?

3. Envision Martha in the kitchen working away and Mary in the den talking and laughing with Jesus. Which sister is more like you? If you are a Martha, what would you like to say in your defense? That said, what are you missing out on by being in the kitchen?

4. When Lazarus was sick with a virus or something and dying, what would your telegram to Jesus have said? Would you have added a bit more detail? How might text messaging change this dynamic today? Do you think Jesus would own a smartphone?

5. Do you find prayer, and praying for people, hard work? Why? Do you think the great saints who prayed hours every day did as well?

6. What secrets of prayer may we learn from Mary and Martha? From their message? From their attitudes towards Jesus?

7. Visualize your intercessory prayers for others as placing people into the giant hands of God. How does that give you peace? How can praying help keep people in God's hands?

8. How does praying for others and placing them in God's hands supply us a "peace" in the midst of challenging days? How can we know a "peace that passes understanding"? Can that peace really "guard" our heart and our worrying mind?

CHAPTER THREE:

1. Have you ever made an "elevator pitch"? What was it and what were you hoping to accomplish?

2. When you need to get an urgent message to someone quickly, how do you do it? How do you mark it as urgent?

3. Have you ever rehearsed your lines for an important conversation in order to get them right? What were the stakes that made you go to this extra effort?

4. Jesus entered the isolation of God willingly; why? Why did he only listen and act on God's command when it came to his words or actions? What would it look like if we paused and listened for God's leading before we acted or spoke? Would we decline more invitations? Would we speak less?

5. Jesus said Lazarus' sickness would result in God's glory. What does that mean? How can Jesus be glorified through something like a coronavirus? Could the same be said when we are sick—"It is not about death but about God's glory"? How might God want to be glorified through us even now?

6. Hypothetically speaking, were the sisters correct to say, "If Jesus were here our brother would not be dying"? Could we say the same thing today, or in the midst of a pandemic, if Jesus were physically present in our pain? If Jesus showed up somewhere would things be made right again?

7. The sisters were convinced that when Jesus returned he would heal Lazarus and make everything right again. Is that your expectation for the return of Jesus Christ today? Why or why not? Are most Christians still awaiting the return of Jesus Christ to make us whole and set the world right again? Or have we given up?

8. The sisters were disappointed in Jesus for not coming sooner—for abandoning them. Have you ever felt abandoned by God? Is it okay to be disappointed in God?

   - Have you ever found God to be *unfair*?
   - Have you ever felt God to be *silent*?
   - Have you ever felt God *hidden* and *distant*?

9. Every worldview or world religion tries to answer the question of suffering and evil in the world. What can we learn from the "partial truth" of other viewpoints? Is there anything there that is true? What can the Hebrew prophets tell us that is still helpful?

10. If you were to frame your doubts and questions about God and Jesus in the "frame" of what you know to be true about them, what would the truths be?

CHAPTER FOUR:

1. How important was it for you to *not* be absent from school? How important was it to be on time? Did you hate "tardies" or did you roll in when you could?

2. How important do you think it is for God *not* to be absent? How important is it to him to not be tardy?

3. If God loves us so much, why does he seem to arrive late, or be absent, when we need him the most? How can that be love?

4. Has God ever been so busy doing other things that he just honestly had no time for us? Why or why not? How can God have the time needed to be there for each of the seven billion-plus who could pray to him at any moment?

5. What was Jesus learning as he waited in spiritual isolation and sacred distancing? What was his quarantine experience designed to do for him? For the sisters?

6. Why did God the Father make Jesus stay in place and serve others when he was ready to go to Bethany?

7. Are there really lessons Jesus had to learn from experience—just like us? How could Jesus "learn obedience through the things he suffered" (Heb 5:8)? Is it possible God asks us to isolate and stay in place for similar reasons?

8. What does it mean that we "grow through what we go through"? How is the quarantine or isolation a place of growth? What is learned there?

9. How is the sacred distancing an opportunity to serve others we find there as well? If Jesus kept working while he waited, how can we do the same?

10. Can we, like Jesus, "wait"—even while still knowing that our situation will not end in defeat? Can we have confidence God will be glorified through our situation as well?

CHAPTER FIVE:

1. Do you like to sleep? Or do you avoid sleep and fight against it? Is it a "hobby" you love to do? What is your funniest story about sleep or "wild dreams"?

2. Are you an early-morning person or a late-night person? When do you do your best work? Why do you think that is so?

3. What was Jesus' attitude toward work? When would he stop doing his work? How did he know when it was time to move on?

4. How will we know when God is calling us to a different task? How can we avoid "running from" something and instead be "called to" something new?

5. In what ways is death like falling asleep? Why do you think this language of "falling asleep" became so important to God's people?

6. Does your computer have a "sleep" mode? In what ways is death like "sleep mode" on your computer?

7. How could Jesus be both sad and glad about the death of Lazarus? What made him glad? Has there ever been a time you were both sad and glad about the death of someone? Why?

8. How do the apostles' actions of returning to Bethany with Jesus model discipleship for us? What does it look like for us to follow Jesus even into danger or death?

9. Jesus is willing to die in order to go and awaken one who is asleep. Is this an image of the gospel as well? Did he die to awaken us?

CHAPTER SIX:

1. What is the most elaborate party you ever attended? What is the most meaningful funeral service you have ever attended? Which event shaped you more? Why? Was Solomon (Eccl 7:1–4) correct?

2. Do you agree that Christianity is different from other world religions because Jesus is alive and can attend a funeral? How does Jesus' resurrection set the truth claims of Christianity apart?

3. What words do you believe would describe Jesus during his two days or working-while-waiting before going to Bethany? What was Jesus learning by not quickly springing to the rescue?

4. Do you think Jesus talked much during the one-day journey once they began to travel to Bethany? Or was he alone in his thoughts? What would you have done as you traveled?

5. What were Martha's first words to Jesus? Were those polite words? Was she really asking, "Why have you forsaken us?" What was she feeling at this time?

6. When Jesus said, "Your brother will rise again," did Martha receive his words as a religious platitude? What platitudes get said often at funerals that do not mean much to those grieving?

7. In saying "I am the resurrection and the life," what was Jesus claiming? Unpack it:

   • I Am

   • The Resurrection

   • The Life

8. Jesus was claiming to be the ultimate meaning of life: life after life after death. Does this mean he was claiming some type of "new creation" for his followers? Does the concept of "metamorphosis" help here?

9. How can Jesus promise we who die will still live and those now living will never die? What does Jesus mean by the word "die," and how does it relate to life with God?

10. Read Romans 8:37–39 and make a list of all the things NOT powerful enough to separate a follower of Jesus from him as resurrection and life. Do you believe it?

CHAPTER SEVEN:

1. Can you think of times as a young child when you genuinely trusted your parents? How did you determine you could really trust them? How had they proved themselves trustworthy?

2. What does it mean to trust God? Is it something we place on a dollar bill or does it mean more? Could it possibly mean that we believe God's plan for our life is better than our own?

3. A father once told Jesus, "I believe, help my unbelief" (Mark 9:24). Is our capacity to trust God like that? Can we both believe and harbor unbelief at the same time? How can we trust Jesus while harboring some doubts as well?

4. Do you blame Martha for blurting out, "If you had been here my brother would not have died"? Do you find this similar to the words of David at the death of Absalom?

5. What did Martha know to be true about Jesus, even though he did not come heal Lazarus? How was this a geopolitical statement of where her trust lay?

6. Mary may have thought she would confront Jesus with her question as Martha had done. Instead she first fell to her knees. Why? Do you have questions you are saving up to ask God when heaven arrives? Do you think you will really ask them or just fall at the feet of Jesus in worship as Mary did?

   - Did worship of Jesus erase her doubts and questions, making them go away?
   - Did worship adjust her own heart? How?

7. Do you have a "bearer group" you know will carry your needs to Jesus in your time of need? Who are they? Where did you find such friends?

8. How do you deal with the seeming unfairness of God? Are you a thinker or a feeler? How does that influence your approach to God in the midst of doubt?

   - Do thinkers try to get all of heaven into their head and get cynical?
   - Do feelers only need to get their head into heaven and just catch a glimpse?

9. Is it okay to tell God you do not understand what he is doing and that you do not like it either? Can such things be said with a worshipful heart and in simple trust? How?

CHAPTER EIGHT:

1. Do you ever laugh at some of the things that now make you cry (a commercial, a song, a poem, a proposal when you do not even know the people)? Are you a crier? Are you the opposite, more of a stoic? Can criers and stoics ever fully understand each other?

2. Why are some men embarrassed to cry? What do tears actually convey about us?

3. Imagine Jesus at the tomb of Lazarus very upset by what he had seen and experienced there. What was it that so disturbed him?

4. Jesus wept. What does this tell us about the humanity of Jesus? What does this say about his deity?

5. How do you respond to the three truths that give us all problems: God is all-good; God is all-powerful; and humankind experiences pain and suffering? How can all three be true? Or are they not all true now?

6. What is similar between Lazarus's burial and a burial today? What is different?

7. How would you respond if Jesus asked you to dig up a buried loved one four days after they died? Do you blame Martha? Wouldn't that be a hard thing to watch unfold?

8. Do tears somehow convey to God our mind, body, soul, and spirit working in tandem to bring our concerns to God? Do you ever long for those tears? How does it feel to know God, through Jesus, shed such tears for those he loves?

CHAPTER NINE:

1. Do you like ghost stories, haunted houses, and scary movies? Does it give you chills when dead bodies and mummies come back to life? Why or why not?

2. Imagine being present as the stone was rolled away from Lazarus's tomb. Would you have imagined Jesus was about to enter it? What would you have thought when Jesus instead yelled, "Lazarus, come out"?

3. Pretend you are an announcer or a reporter describing what you see and hear. How would you tell this story? How would you give a moment by moment description of the details?

4. How would you explain Hades, the "waiting place," to a young person age twelve? What is it like? Are the faithful asleep there?

5. Is resurrection much like the end result of *metamorphosis?* If so, is Hades a bit like going into a cocoon to sleep? Do we enter into death in order to be raised again as something else—something more beautiful? Discuss the similarities and differences.

6. Lazarus came out of the tomb and then had to "take off" his grave clothes and "put on" new clothes. How is this similar (see Eph 4:22–24) to an unbeliever becoming a follower of Jesus? What role does Christian baptism play in this process?

7. Explain each response below. What would make someone who experienced and encountered the Lazarus story . . .

    • put their trust in Jesus?

    • want to get rid of Jesus?

    • need to honor Jesus in a significant way?

8. Describe the sights and smells of Martha's elaborate dinner . . . and then of Mary's extravagant gift. What would that moment have been like to an invited guest? What did that moment mean to Jesus?

CHAPTER TEN:

1. Have you ever attended a parade? What made the atmosphere so exciting? Have you ever been in parade? What was it like to be "inside the ropes"?

2. Why did the crowds line the road with palm branches and singing as Jesus entered Jerusalem? What were they so excited about? In what capacity were they welcoming Jesus? Does that kind of enthusiasm last long?

3. Would you have enjoyed being present when Jesus cleared the temple? What action by Jesus most surprises you? Why was Jesus so concerned about prayer—especially the prayers of foreigners?

4. Why does power seem to corrupt good people? How did power cause the religious leaders to make evil decisions?

5. Imagine Jesus showing up to teach in the temple the day after clearing the temple. Would there be large crowds to hear him? Why do you think Jesus had such wise responses to those trying to trap him? Where did his words come from anyway?

6. What made the disciples bicker about who would be the greatest? Are we like that? What makes us crave being a little better than everyone else?

7. How did Jesus washing feet give a final response to the disciples' quest for power? Is there *really* a blessing in being a servant to all? Explain.

8. How can Jesus be such a non-anxious presence in the garden of Gethsemane and on trial before Pilate and Caiaphas? What did he have that no one else did? Is there a secret there for our anxiety also?

9. Which of Jesus' seven sayings from the cross is most significant for you? Why?

10. How did David's words then become Jesus' words over a thousand years later? In what ways had God the Father *really forsaken* Jesus? Why?

CHAPTER ELEVEN:

1. Is there someone about whom you can say, "I see myself in them"? Who is it? Do the similarities between you ever seem uncanny?

2. What makes the love of a best friend so significant? How can you tell the difference between a "casual friend" and one approaching the "best friend" category?

3. What makes the love of a father for an only son so significant? Is there a sense that the father always sees himself in the son? Is that good, bad, what?

4. If you were Jesus' closest friend, how would you feel? What character qualities do you think Jesus would want in a best friend?

5. How did Lazarus's death prepare Jesus to better understand his own pending death? What feelings that Lazarus once felt became Jesus'

own at the cross? Similarly, could Jesus' death in some way help us prepare for our own?

6. In what ways was Lazarus the "schoolmaster" for Jesus throughout his death? In what ways was Lazarus a counselor or guide? How did Lazarus play a role like Moses and Elijah had done for Jesus?

7. As Lazarus had heard Jesus' loud cry from his place in Hades, Jesus would later descend into Hades himself (see the Apostles' Creed) as well. What did Jesus do in Hades? What was he announcing?

8. Did Jesus want to understand Lazarus's death in order to better navigate his own? Do we want to know Jesus' death to better understand our own (see Phil 3:10–11)?

CHAPTER TWELVE:

1. Personally, are you wired more to the rational side or the emotional side? What gifts do you bring to a church community because of your wiring?

2. Read Romans 12:3–8. Imagine Martha without Mary or vice versa; what would be missing from their home? Imagine if your church were filled with only people like you; what would you be missing? How can you learn to be grateful for the differences brought by different types of people?

3. Think about your church community. Is it a place where Jesus would feel welcome? Could you say, "There is more love per square inch here than anywhere else I know"? Why or why not?

4. How can we as a church *accompany* each other through the hard times? What does it require to engage and absorb some of the suffering of others?

5. How important is intercessory prayer to your church family? To you personally? Do you have names you are constantly praying for and placing in Jesus' hands? Is there a team of people praying for those in need?

6. Think about the excuses the sisters could have used for not sending a telegram of intercession to Jesus. Which excuses sound like your own

excuses to not pray more? Does it surprise you that Jesus knows all your unsaid prayers too?

7. Jesus' delay sowed doubt among the sisters of three kinds. Is doubt prevalent among us today as well? How can we be real about our doubts while still striving to live by faith? Does God mind it when we doubt? Could it be God's tool to increase faith?

8. Is there really such thing as a "ministry of absence"? What can make absence an open space for the love of God to fill?

9. What does it look like for a faith community to "grieve with hope"? Is there still sorrow? Is there certainty? Is the loved one who dies still alive to Jesus and to God? How?

10. What can we learn about the great feast to come from the feast Martha threw to honor Jesus? What does it reveal to us about the Eucharist or the Lord's Supper we observe in the meantime?

CHAPTER THIRTEEN:

1. Have you had a "conversion experience" in coming to know Jesus as Lord? What do you remember about it?

2. How important is "confessing Jesus" to our faith story? Is there something about making a public declaration that shapes us—do the words become more real?

3. How serious do you think Lazarus was about the consequences of sin after his trip to Hades and time spent there? Do you think he hated sin?

4. In some small way, was Lazarus's time under the waters of baptism a bit like self-isolation? Like a burial?

5. If you asked Lazarus what God was doing at Pentecost, what would he say? What did it all mean?

6. Read Acts 2:42–48. How did these practices help form Lazarus and others in the early church?

7. How central was prayer and the Lord's Prayer to Lazarus and the early followers? What can we learn from their prayer life?

8. Why was a commitment to holiness so important? Who was watching them? Who was looking for a reason to discount them?

9. Do you think Lazarus would have really changed his business practices like in our story? What key aspects of Lazarus's business dealings could help us in ours?

10. Lazarus worked for the renewal of creation—especially in Bethany. In what ways should we be about the renewal of the creation until the new heaven and new earth are revealed?

11. What would you do today if you knew Jesus was coming back tomorrow? Who would you talk to today? What actions would you engage in to make the new creation more fitting for the return of Jesus?

Acknowledgments

The Christian Church in its practical relation to my soul is a living teacher, not a dead one. It not only certainly taught me yesterday, but will almost certainly teach me to-morrow. . . . Plato has told you a truth; but Plato is dead. Shakespeare has startled you with an image; but Shakespeare will not startle you with any more. But imagine what it would be to live with such men still living, to know that Plato might break out with an original lecture to-morrow, or that at any moment Shakespeare might shatter everything with a single song. The man who lives in contact with what he believes to be a living Church is a man always expecting to meet Plato and Shakespeare to-morrow at breakfast. He is always expecting to see some truth that he has never seen before.[184]

—G. K. CHESTERTON

I AM GRATEFUL TO be a part of a living church where fresh insights from the Spirit come to God's people every day. The church that has shaped and formed me has helped to shape this book. I want to also think Audible for supplying me with some excellent research assistants I have listened to over and over again. In chronological order these men include: George Mac-Donald, G. K. Chesterton, C. S. Lewis, Alister McGrath, and N. T. Wright. This book would not be near the theological work it has become without their assistance, especially C. S. Lewis and N. T. Wright.

If you find anything in this book that would please Shakespeare, the credit for my attention to poetry resides with: Ed Madden, Judy Brooks, Robert Hicks, Jeff Wheeler, Courtney Rainwater, Shane Neal, Denny Loyd, John Parker, and my preaching hero, Peter Marshall. If you find anything in this work that would please Plato that credit would go to: Billy Abraham, Caleb Clanton, Rubel Shelly, David Young, Bill Marquette, or Mark Lanier.

I am grateful to Fran Armour for typing an original draft that became the skeleton for this book; there is no finer servant. I esteem highly my friends and family for their support: J. P. and Marge, Dave and Diana, Jim and Dana, John and Claire, all with the last name "Sager." Jamie and Harrison Goad and Jerry, Anne, Brison, and Rachel Matula have also shown great encouragement. I'm grateful for my "Bethany" in College Mound, Texas, with Hugh McClung and his sister Laura, Wynne and Liddy Breeden. I am immensely grateful for my former church family at Preston Road in Dallas, with special mention to Pat and Pete Schenkel, Jeff and Cara Wheeler, Jim Barnett, Ron Unkefer, Pete Dysert, Cooter Hale, Jane Fitch, Barbara Perkins, the Branches, Bairds, Heards, Stukalins, and my Ladies' Bible Class friends. I am also grateful for the very supportive shepherds at the Green Hills Church of Christ for their encouragement and kindness—and for their willingness to financially sponsor this project. These men are true servants and amaze me with their Christlikeness.

I would like to thank the professors who poured into me throughout the years: Tom Geer, Charles Siburt, Jack Reese, Leonard Allen, Everett Ferguson, John Willis, David Wray, Ian Fair, Wendell Broom, Carl Brecheen, Paul Faulkner, Gaston Tarbet, Billy Abraham, and Larry James. I would also like to thank several college presidents for their friendship and support: Gerald Turner, Royce Money, Andy Westmoreland, Bruce McLarty, Harold Hazelip, Michael Adams, and my boss, Randy Lowry. In addition, I would like to thank my supportive colleagues at Lipscomb University: Kent Gallaher, Alan Bradshaw, Richard Goode, Jon Lowrance, David Holmes, Caleb Clanton, JP Conway, Steve Joiner, Junior High, Walt Leaver, Carl McKelvey, Dean Leonard Allen, John Mark Hicks, Richard Hughes, Earl Lavender, Lauren White, Rhonda Lowry, Philip Camp, Mike Williams, Claire Frederick, Randy Gill, Lee Camp, Matt Paden, Ciera Cypert, Nan Hensley, Leslie Landiss, Keely Hagan, and a special thanks to Provost Craig Bledsoe.

I am most grateful to Joe Shulam, Wendell Broom, and Dorothy Rooker who introduced me to Israel and my first visit to Bethany in 1987. I am equally grateful to Bill and Shelva Biggs, Ken and Desiree Barnes, and the Melissa Renee Barnes Trust and the Lanier Theological Library that support my current teaching in Israel—and to Father Justin, who is my friend in the Sinai. I am also grateful to my guide and friends in Israel: Hannah Kovner, the late Shukry Lawrence, and Henry Lawrence. I am appreciative

ACKNOWLEDGMENTS

of ministry friends across the country that have been of mutual support throughout the years: Buddy Bell, Milton Jones, Rick Atchley, Randy Harris, David Young, Greg Allen, Chris Altrock, Hal Runkel, Chris Seidman, Jason Henderson, and Bobby Harrington.

I want to thank Max Lucado, Kyle Idleman, Mark Lanier, Steve Gladen, Rick Rusaw, George Goldman, Dave Schroeder, and David Capes for a willingness to engage with this manuscript to make it better. Thank you Neika Stephens for your keen eye and wise counsel in editing. And thank you, Ward Baker, for championing this manuscript in the halls of DC.

Thank you, Anna and Will Sager, for making life fun and for your patience and encouragement as this book was spread out on the living room table for way too long. Thank you, Mom and Dad, for your support throughout this journey. Suzanne, you are my Martha and Mary rolled into one, and I am grateful for your warmth and wit.

W. Scott Sager

Endnotes

1. Lewis, *Mere Christianity*, 176–77.

2. Throughout the book I use the biblical tools of historical, exegetical, and theological interpretation, but I fill in the gaps in the story in an "imaginative" way. Imagining Jesus absorbing the grief of others.

3. Donne, "Meditation I."

4. This chapter first appeared in *An Honest Cry: Sermons from the Psalms in Honor of Prentice A. Meador Jr.* and is used by permission.

5. COVID-19 insight: They say nothing stings like the death of a child, but those who say such things are wrong. Missing the funeral after the death of a child stings far more—for there was no parting word, no formal goodbye, and no closure.

6. "Gospel" means "good news" and is one of four lengthy writings about Jesus. These writings tell of his origin, his ministry, his teaching, and his death, burial, and resurrection at the cross. John is this author's favorite and he hopes you'll read it straight through one day.

7. The New Testament city named "Bethany" actually means "House of Affliction" and was probably the Old Testament city of Anathoth. Today the town is called, "El 'Azariyeh"—a name derived from its most famous inhabitant, Lazarus.

8. This story is found in Luke 10:38–42.

9. We have no record of Jesus' father Joseph after Jesus turned twelve. Most scholars believe he died young and Jesus took over the carpentry shop until his brothers were old enough to do so.

10. See Mark 2:1–12 for this wonderful story in full detail.

11. See Luke 13:16.

12. Lewis, *Problem of Pain*, 91.

13. See Gen 18:27–28.

14. Foster, *Prayer*, 191.

15. See Ps 121:4.

16. See Rom 8:34.

17. See Heb 7:25.

18. See Luke 11:5–13.

19. See Luke 18:1–8.

20. Theophan the Recluse, taken from Nouwen, *Living Reminder*, 71.

21. Romanus, "Kontakion on the Raising of Lazarus," 15.2–3, in Elowsky, *John 11–21*, 2.

22. See John 5:19.

23. See Ps 116:15.

24. I am grateful to Yancey, *Disappointment with God*, 36 for these categories.

25. Lewis, *Grief Observed*, 3.

26. Yancey, *Where Is God When It Hurts?* 16.

27. See Hab 2:20.

28. Dickinson, "Bustle in a House."

29. See John 11:5–6.

30. See Heb 5:8.

31. See Pss 40:1 and 27:14.

32. See Ps 130:5–6.

33. See Isa 30:18.

34. See Ps 121:1.

35. In Gen 1:5 and on five other occasions in the chapter we discover that "evening" comes before "morning" as darkness comes before the dawn.

36. Madden, "Thirst."

37. See John 13:30.

38. See Matt 5:14–16.

39. See John 8:12.

40. Augustine, "Tractates on the Gospel of John," 273 (49:9).

41. See Dan 12:2.

42. See Mark 5:39.

43. See Acts 13:36.

44. Wright, *Surprised by Hope*, 171.

45. Chrysologus, "Sermon 63," in Elowsky, *John 11–21*, 5.

46. See John 11:14.

47. Many scholars believe Peter was absent from this story, perhaps visiting his family for some reason. This accounts for the absence of the Lazarus story from Mark's Gospel and explains why Thomas has taken Peter's role in the lead.

48. Bonhoeffer, *Cost of Discipleship*, 89.

49. The word for witness in the Greek is *martureo*, from which the word *martyr* derives.

50. Shelley, "Queen Mab."

51. See Luke 4:18–19.

52. See Heb 5:8–9.

53. *Jehovah-Rophe* means the "God who heals" and is mentioned in Exod 15:26 where God promises to heal and deliver Israel.

54. See Acts 1:21–26.

55. This means Lazarus died the same day the messenger arrived to meet Jesus. Figuring it was one day of travel for the messenger, two days of waiting by Jesus, and one day of travel by Jesus to Bethany, that equals four days.

56. See John 11:19.

57. See fuller poem, "No Man Is an Island," at end of this chapter.

58. At Jesus' second coming, his appearance, those who are Jesus' followers will rise to meet him in the air. From there, they will then usher Jesus' into the New Jerusalem coming down from heaven where they will live and even reign with Jesus on earth. See N. T. Wright's insights: *Surprised by Hope*, 128–33.

59. Lewis, *Grief Observed*, 25.

60. See Gen 14:22.

61. See Exod 3:14.

62. Athanasius, "Homily on the Resurrection of Lazarus," in Bernardin, "Resurrection of Lazarus," 262–90.

63. Wright, *Surprised by Hope*, 36; see also 168–69.

64. Wright, *Surprised by Hope*, 37.

65. See Rom 8:9–11.

66. Wright, *Surprised by Hope*, 36; see discussion on 35–40, 169–70.

67. The Hindu religion has as its "highest state" the dissolution of a person back into the cosmos, a giving up of self to be united with creation. This is called *moksha*, or liberation.

68. See Ps 116:15.

69. See Rom 8:38–39.

70. Donne, "Meditation XVII."

71. See 2 Cor 1:20.

72. See 2 Cor 1:20.

73. "Pisteuo," 849.

74. See John 20:31.

75. See Deut 18:18.

76. See Gen 49:10; 2 Sam 7:12; Pss 2:1–6, 110:1–4; Isa 9:6–7, 11:1, 61:1–2; Dan 7:13–14; Mic 5:2; Zech 9:9, among others.

77. See Matt 22:15–22.

78. Origen, "Fragments on the Gospel of John," in Smith, *Ante-Nicene Exegesis of the Gospels*, 4:170–71.

79. Origen, "Fragments on the Gospel of John," in Smith, *Ante-Nicene Exegesis of the Gospels*, 4:170–71.

80. Morris, *Reflections on the Gospel of John*, 410.

81. See John 2.

82. Lovat, *Life of St. Teresa*, 548.

83. Poe, "Alone."

84. See Eccl 3:1–4, 10–11.

85. See John 11:33.

86. See 1 Thess 4:13.

87. See John 1:37–39.

88. See 2 Sam 6:14–15.

89. See 2 Sam 6:16.

90. See Luke 19:41.

91. See Mark 6:3.

92. The authenticity of the tomb dates back to Eusebius in AD 330 and the church on the site to Jerome in AD 390. The church was later adapted to the Mosque of al-Uzair in AD 1384.

93. The ossuary of Caiaphas the high priest and twelve others of his family have been found from this period, and his ossuary is now located in the Israel Museum.

94. See John 17.

95. Foster, *Prayer*, 41.

96. See Job 16:20.

97. See Isa 16:9.

98. See Jer 9:1 and Lam 2:18.

99. See Pss 6:6, 56:8, 42:3, 119:136.

100. See Matt 5:4 and Luke 6:21.

101. Foster, *Prayer*, 39.

102. See Heb 5:7.

103. See Rom 8:26–27.

104. I am especially thankful to Richard Foster's work, *Prayer*, for the material on the Prayer of Tears.

105. Van Dyke, "Katrina's Sundial."

106. Athanasius, "Homily on the Resurrection of Lazarus," in Elowsky, *John 11–21*, 26.

107. See Ps 22:22–24.

108. Gregory of Nyssa, "On the Making of Man," 416–17.

109. Hippolytus, "On the Gospel of John," in Elowsky, *John 11–21*, 30.

110. Gregory of Nyssa, "On the Making of Man," 416–17

111. See 1 Pet 3:19.

112. See Luke 16:19–31.

113. Phillips, "Hades."

114. Lewis, *Great Divorce*; see chapters 7–9.

115. See 2 Cor 3:18.

116. See 2 Cor 5:1–4.

117. The Greek word for "cemetery" is *koimeterion*, and it means a "sleeping or resting place." Our word for "dormitory" comes from it. This is the idea Jesus is conveying in John 14 in stating, "In my Father's house are many rooms."

118. Andrew of Crete, "Homilies on Lazarus and Palm Sunday," in Elowsky, *John 11–21*, 29.

119. See John 11:45.

120. See John 11:18–19.

121. Brown, *Gospel according to John*, 434.

122. Adler and Hirsch, "Shemoneh 'Esreh."

123. Adler and Hirsch, "Shemoneh 'Esreh."

124. See John 11:46–47.

125. See John 11:48.

126. See John 11:49–50.

127. See John 11:51–52.

128. Cyril of Alexandria, "Gospel according to St. John," in Elowsky, *John 11–21*, 22.

129. Theodore of Mopsuestia, *Early Christian Studies*, 5:12:19, in Elowsky, *John 11–21*, 49.

130. Amazingly, Judas Iscariot would sit in this seat at the Last Supper until the time he left to betray Jesus.

131. See Luke 9:30–31.

132. See Rev 2:17.

133. See John 12:11.

134. Chrysostom, "Homilies on the Gospel of John," in Elowsky, *John 11–21*, 50.

135. Donne, "Death Be Not Proud."

136. See John 12:17.

137. See John 12:19.

138. See Matt 26:3–5.

139. See Mark 10:35.

140. See John 13:14–17.

141. See Mark 14:25.

142. See Luke 22:48.

143. See Luke 22:53.

144. See John 18: 20–21 and John 18:23.

145. See Ps 23.

146. Isaac Watts, "When I Survey the Wondrous Cross," 1707.

147. See 1 Pet 3:18–21 for information on Jesus' proclamation of good news to the spirits in prison.

148. See Mark 1:11.

149. See Mark 9:7.

150. See Philippians 3:10–11 for this religious imagery.

151. See Rev. 20:6.

152. Francis of Assisi, "All Creatures of our God and King."

153. See John 17.

154. See John 4:32–38.

155. See Luke 18:1–8.

156. See 1 Cor 16:22 for this Aramaic prayer of the early church.

157. Gothard, *Institute of Basic Youth Conflicts*, 149–50.

158. See Matt 18:18.

159. Augustine, "Sermon 67," in Elowsky, *John 11–21*, 31.

160. William Walsham How, "For All the Saints," 1864.

161. Perhaps even Martha and Mary, but for sure the women mentioned in Luke 8.

162. A pesher is a rereading of a Psalm or sacred text discovering within it illusions and images of Jesus' messiahship. The earliest Christians were constantly discovering words about Jesus in Old Testament texts. Lazarus would have been especially amazed as he read Psalms 6:5, 17:15, 18:4–6, 88:10–12, and 116:1–4, which asked questions he could answer as one back from the dead.

163. Symeon, "Hymn 1," in McGuckin, "Symeon the New Thologian's Hymns."

164. See Irenaeus, "Against Heresies," 5:13.1, in Elowsky, *John 11–21*, 31.

165. See Revelation 12 for a description of this cosmic battle fought in and around the coming of Jesus.

166. See Rom 6:1–11 for the textual explanation behind this prayer.

167. See Gal 3:26–29 for the explanation of these comments.

168. From the beginning of the church in Acts 2:9–11 we see that some form of Arabic and Chinese were languages spoken at Pentecost, as well as Greek, Latin, Hebrew, and probably Spanish as well.

169. See Col 3:1–11 for this explanation of the Christian walk after baptism.

170. See Acts 2:42 for this basic disciple-making strategy given to the apostles first through the modeling of Jesus and then through his Great Commission in Matt 28:18–20.

171. See Dave Clayton's brief but helpful guide, *Revival Starts Here*, at discipleship.org to learn helpful tips to start a movement of prayer and fasting in your spiritual community.

172. See www.awakennashville.com for a model on praying and fasting for your city as well.

173. To learn more about the impact bosses can have in the workplace visit the "T-Factor" at t-factor.com where Frank Harrison, Dave Katz, and the team at Coca-Cola Consolidated share their amazing stories of spiritual transformation of a significant business venture.

174. See Luke 4:16–21.

175. The word for "witness" in the Greek is *marturia*, and one who is Jesus' ultimate witness is then called a "martyr"—taken from the same word.

176. This *is* actually what Martin Luther suggested as a final act before Jesus' return.

177. Donne, "Expostulation XXI."

178. Thanks to Rabbi Herschel for this insight.

179. Watson, *Called and Committed*, 83.

180. Gordon, *Quiet Talks on Prayer*, 4.

181. Yancy, *Where Is God When It Hurts?* 86.

182. Lewis, *Grief Observed*, 26.

183. Bonhoeffer, *Cost of Discipleship*, 89.

184. Chesterton, *Orthodoxy*, 118–19.

Bibliography

Adler, Cyrus, and Emil G. Hirsch. "Shemoneh 'Esreh." In *The Jewish Encyclopedia*, edited by Isidore Singer. New York: Funk & Wagnalls, 1906. https://www.jewishencyclopedia.com/articles/1398-amidah.

Augustine. "Tractates on the Gospel of St. John." In *Nicene and Post-Nicene Fathers 2*, edited by Philip Schaff, 7:270–78. Buffalo, NY: Christian Literature, 1994.

Bernardin, Joseph B. "The Resurrection of Lazarus." *American Journal of Semitic Languages and Literature* 57.3 (1940) 262–90.

Bonhoeffer, Dietrich. *The Cost of Discipleship*. New York: Simon & Schuster, 1995.

Brown, Raymond. *The Gospel According to John I–XII*. Anchor Bible 29. New York: Doubleday, 1966.

Chesterton, Gilbert K. *Orthodoxy*. Sioux Falls, SD: Nu-Vision, 2009.

Clayton, Dave. *Revival Starts Here*. Nashville: HIM Publications, 2018.

Dickinson, Emily. "The Bustle in a House." In *The Complete Poems of Emily Dickinson*, 330. Boston: Little, Brown, 1924. Bartleby.com, 2000. www.bartleby.com/113/.

Donne, John. "Death Be Not Proud." In *The Poems of John Donne*, edited by Herbert J. C. Grierson, 1:326. Oxford: Clarendon, 1912.

———. "Expostulation XII." In *Devotions upon Emergent Occasions*, 140–41. 1624. Urbana, IL: Project Gutenberg, 2007. http://www.gutenberg.org/ebooks/23772.

———. "Meditation I." In *Devotions upon Emergent Occasions*, 8. 1624. Urbana, IL: Project Gutenberg, 2007. http://www.gutenberg.org/ebooks/23772.

———. "Meditation XVII: No Man Is an Island." In *Devotions upon Emergent Occasions*, 108–9. 1624. Urbana, IL: Project Gutenberg, 2007. http://www.gutenberg.org/ebooks/23772.

Elowsky, Joel C., ed. *John 11–21*. Ancient Christian Commentary on Scripture NT IVb. Downers Grove: InterVarsity, 2007.

Foster, Richard. *Prayer: Finding the Heart's True Home*. San Francisco: HarperSanFrancisco, 1992.

Francis of Assisi. "All Creatures of our God and King." Paraphrased by William H. Draper. Hymnary.org. 1225.

Gordon, S. D. *Quiet Talks on Prayer*. London: Revell, 1904.

Gothard, Bill. *Institute of Basic Youth Conflicts: Research in Principles of Life*. N.p.: Institute in Basic Youth Conflicts, 1979.

Gregory of Nyssa. "On the Making of Man." In *Nicene and Post-Nicene Fathers 2*, edited by Philip Schaff, 5:386–427. Buffalo, NY: Christian Literature, 1994.

Irenaeus. "Against Heresies." In *The Apostolic Fathers with Justin Martyr and Irenaeus*, translated by Cleveland Cox, 66–72. Peabody, MA: Hendrickson, 1994.

Lewis, C. S. *The Great Divorce*. 1946. Reprint, San Francisco: HarperSanFrancisco, 1973.

———. *A Grief Observed*. San Francisco: HarperSanFrancisco, 1996.

———. *Mere Christianity*. 1952. Reprint, New York: Harper Collins, 2001.

———. *The Problem of Pain*. New York: Harper Collins, 2002.

Lovat, Alice Neid Deundell. *The Life of St. Teresa: Of the Order of Mount Carmel*. London: Herbert & Daniel, 1912.

Madden, Ed. "Thirst." In *Ark*, 73. Little Rock: Sibling Rivalry, 2016.

Morris, Leon. *Reflections on the Gospel of John*. Vol. 4: *Crucified and Risen: John 17–21*. Grand Rapids: Baker, 1988.

Nouwen, Henry. *The Living Reminder*. New York: Seabury, 1977.

Phillips, Timothy R. "Hades." In *Baker's Evangelical Dictionary of Biblical Theology*, edited by Walter A. Elwell, n.p. Baker Reference Library. Grand Rapids: Baker, 1996. Online edition.

"Pisteuo." In *The Theological Dictionary of the New Testament*, edited by Gerhard Kittel and Gerhard Friedrich, translated by Geoffrey W. Bromiley, 6:174, 849. Grand Rapids: Eerdmans, 1964.

Poe, Edgar Allan. "Alone." In *American Poetry: The 19th Century*, 1:552. New York: Literary Classics, 1993.

Sager, W. Scott. *An Honest Cry: Sermons from the Psalms in Honor of Prentice A. Meador Jr.* Abilene, TX: Leafwood, 2010.

McGuckin, John Anthony. "Symeon the New Theologian's Hymns of Divine Eros: A Neglected Masterpiece of the Christian Mystical Tradition." *Spiritus* 5 (2005) 182–202.

Shelley, Percy Bysshe. "Queen Mab." In *The Complete Poetical Works*. New York: Houghton Mifflin, 1901. Bartleby.com, 1999. www.bartleby.com/139/.

Smith, Harold, trans. *Ante-Nicene Exegesis of the Gospels*. 6 vols. London: SPCK, 1928–29.

Tolkien, J. R. R. *The Letters of J. R. R. Tolkien*. Edited by Humphrey Carpenter with the assistance of Christopher Tolkien. Sydney: Allen & Unwin: 2014.

Van Dyke, Henry. "Katrina's Sundial." In *Music and Other Poems*. 1904. Urbana, IL: Project Gutenberg, 2013. http://www.gutenberg.org/ebooks/3525.

Watson, David. *Called and Committed*. Wheaton: Harold Shaw, 1982.

Wright, N. T. *Surprised by Hope*. New York: HarperOne, 2008.

Yancey, Philip. *Disappointment with God*. Grand Rapids: Zondervan, 1997.

———. *Where Is God When It Hurts?* Grand Rapids: Zondervan, 2002.